Let's All Play

Activities for Communication, Language and Literacy

RESOURCES AVAILABLE FOR DOWNLOAD

All online resources included in this book are available at http://www.continuumbooks.com/resources/9780826423948.

Please visit this link to register with us to receive your password and access to the downloadable online resources.

If you experience any problems accessing the online resources, please contact Continuum at info@continuumbooks.com

Let's All Play

Activities for Communication, Language and Literacy

JENNY ROE

continuum

Continuum International Publishing Group
The Tower Building   80 Maiden Lane, Suite 704
11 York Road   New York, NY 10038
London, SE1 7NX

www.continuumbooks.com

© Jenny Roe 2008

British Library Cataloguing-in-Publication Data
A catalogue record for this book is available from the British Library.

ISBN: 9-7808-2642-394-8 (paperback)
Library of Congress Cataloguing-in-Publication Data
A catalog record of this title is available from the Library of Congress.

Illustrations by Clare Jarvis
Typeset by Ben Cracknell Studios | www.benstudios.co.uk
Printed and bound in Great Britain by Ashford Colour Press Ltd, Gosport, Hampshire.

Contents

Acknowledgements

Many people have been generous with their advice and help in writing this book. I would particularly like to thank my family and friends for their continued support and belief in this book and me, especially to Christine Roe for her wonderful creativity, support and constant encouragement.

I would like to thank my editor Christina Garbutt for her enthusiasm and for sharing my vision in this book. Also thanks to Clare Jarvis for illustrating this book so beautifully in our first collaborative project together. Hopefully the first of many!

Thanks also to my colleagues who provided their feedback and encouragement including: Ruth Zimmerman, Joanne Munro, Ingrid Turner and Louise Mart.

Many thanks to the organizations who have been more than generous in providing feedback and their expertise and knowledge in supporting a range of children including: the National Deaf Children's Society, the National Blind Children's Society, the Royal National Institute of Blind People, the Ace Centre North, the British Dyslexia Association and the National Autistic Society.

Introduction

This book is packed with enjoyable, easy-to-do literacy activities for young children. It is a resource for anyone working with nursery, reception or pre-school children in any early years setting.

The activities in this book aim to build on good practice which will already be familiar in many settings. This book provides fun, stimulating and inclusive ideas suitable for a range of children including those with special educational needs (SEN) and those learning English as an additional language (EAL).

How do children learn?

Communication, language and literacy activity needs to interest and motivate young children. Furthermore, all children have a natural desire to learn and should be active participants in their own development and learning. The principles of this book, which outline how all young children learn, are as follows:

- Multi-sensory learning – children will benefit from activities that evoke all the senses to create a rich, meaningful and varied learning environment. This supports the many different learning styles children have and is especially effective for children with SEN or those learning EAL.
- Play – children must be motivated and demonstrate a willingness to become involved in their own learning. This is best achieved through play.
- Meaningful contexts – children's learning needs to be developed in a variety of meaningful and practical contexts that are relevant to their everyday lives. For example, use real-life oranges not plastic food. This aspect is an important factor for children learning EAL or for those with learning difficulties as it helps them to better understand and apply what they are learning.
- Repetition – revisiting an enjoyable activity makes it familiar to children, increasing their confidence and sense of control over their own learning.
- Observation – children need opportunities to watch and listen, both to adults and each other. This helps them to understand an activity, discuss their ideas and use other people's ideas to develop their own.
- Communication – children use 'talk' to support all areas of learning, both to each other and to adults. Language enables children to clarify their ideas and actions, and helps them to understand and process their learning. Children with limited language or those who have a speech or hearing impairment may be reluctant to engage in conversations. They must be nurtured by adults who can welcome and encourage the pre-requisites to spoken communication, including using facial expressions, gestures, actions and alternative methods of communication such as signing, Braille and picture communication (see Supporting children – additional information).

Parents as partners

Children arrive at their early years setting with a wealth of prior learning and experiences from home. Future learning and development has to take into account the integral role parents and carers have in their child's learning.

Invite families into your setting to share their knowledge. Talk to families and carers about the activities you are doing, so that they can continue to support their child's learning at home.

Each chapter provides ideas for parents as partners, which aim to promote inclusive practice for all families.

Unique children

It is important to recognize and support differences as outlined in the Early Years Foundation Stage's (EYFS) 'Unique child' by individualizing teaching and learning. You may work with a child who is experiencing difficulties and not making adequate progress. A child may require additional support for many reasons, including: their age; limited prior knowledge and understanding; they may have SEN or may be learning EAL. Alternatively you may work with a child who learns quickly, and easily becomes bored and frustrated when activities do not challenge them.

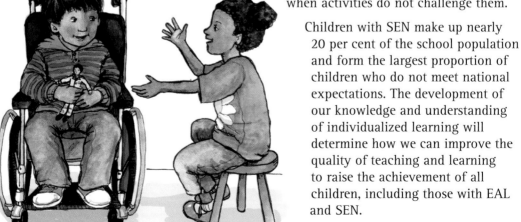

Children with SEN make up nearly 20 per cent of the school population and form the largest proportion of children who do not meet national expectations. The development of our knowledge and understanding of individualized learning will determine how we can improve the quality of teaching and learning to raise the achievement of all children, including those with EAL and SEN.

While children learning EAL may require support, they do not fall into a special needs category. This distinction must be acknowledged in your planning and teaching. Children learning EAL should develop their language skills readily if provided with the support, tools and environment to encourage this.

Some children may have SEN resulting in difficulties in communication and interaction, cognition and learning, behavioural, emotional and social development or sensory or physical needs. These children may have some difficulties in acquiring and retaining new skills as a result of specific challenges presented by their disability.

Each activity provides ideas for differentiating the session, to provide further support for some children or to challenge the more able. Additional information on supporting specific groups of children in 'Supporting children' as well as links to 'Further reading and information' can be found at the back of this book.

It is paramount that each child is recognized as unique and may require individualized support from specialists, professionals and therapists. While this book may not provide all the answers, it aims to provide those working with young children with a starting point and to inspire them to think creatively about differentiating activities to meet all needs.

How to use this book

This book is organized into five topic-themed chapters: 'Animals', 'Food Glorious Food', 'All About Me', 'Opposites' and 'Houses and Homes'. Each chapter begins with a taster paragraph and a list of contents of activities which provide broad and balanced coverage of the six strands of communication, language and literacy as defined in the EYFS which are handwriting, writing, reading, linking sounds and letters, communication for language and communication for thinking.

Each chapter has an introduction which suggests ideas for role-play areas, songs, hands-on learning, parents as partner home activities and links with the Early Learning Goals in other areas of the curriculum such as personal, social and emotional development, and knowledge and understanding of the world.

An example activity

You will need – this lists the resources for the activity. The book is designed to be used with simple materials and resources. However to save time and effort there is a wealth of online material including images, text extracts, audio and writing skeletons. These are available to use on a whiteboard or to print. Activities which have inline resources will be marked with 'Online resources available'.

Vocabulary – these are some of the keywords you may use during the activity. They include everyday words as well as common or high-frequency words listed in the National Literacy Strategy Framework for reception-aged children. The words can be used to expand children's vocabulary as well as focusing their learning by encouraging them to repeat and use the words for themselves.

Activity – the description of activity designed for small groups of four to five children.

LANGUAGE FOR THINKING

ACTIVITY 35
Doctor! Doctor!

Vocabulary
medicine, injection, bandage, ill, healthy

Introduce the doctor's role-play area to the children by modelling to them appropriate language, gestures and actions. For example, 'Good morning, what seems to be the problem?' Ask the children What do doctors do? How do they make us better? Who has been to the doctor?

Encourage the children to take on different roles and act out imaginary scenarios in character using the dolls and teddies. Encourage them to talk about what is happening.

You will need
A doctors' role-play area, including doctors' instruments such as stethoscope, bandages, play thermometer, syringe, medicine and so on.

You will also need
Leaflets, posters and notices, waiting room area, dolls, teddies, magazines for the waiting room, reception desk and equipment.

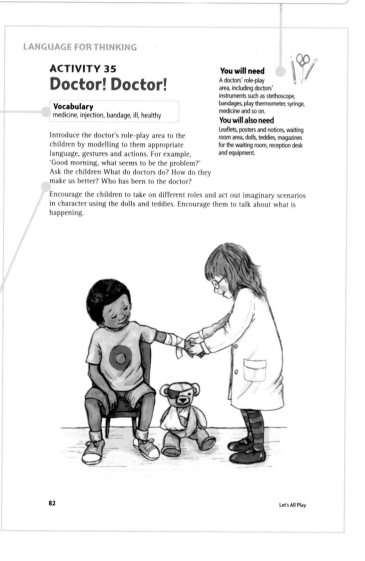

82

Let's All Play

Meeting different learners' needs – this section suggests ways of varying the activity for different age ranges and abilities as well as, where possible, for children learning EAL and for those with special needs.

Learning steps – this section outlines significant steps leading to the Communication, Language and Literacy Early Learning Goals as outlined within 'Development matters' in the EYFS. By recognizing the early steps of learning leading towards the Early Learning Goals, this section helps to recognize the different goals that children who need support will be working towards. The bullet points show a progression of steps starting from easier to more challenging goals leading to the Early Learning Goals indicated by red bullets.

Meeting different learners' needs

Support some children by providing them with a running commentary to describe what you are doing, using gestures, actions and props to give added meaning. Provide them with props to support their role-play skills. Encourage the children to use all of their senses during the activity, such as listening for a heart beat, touching and exploring different role-play resources and smelling different safe medical creams such as Sudacrem. Voice output devices and symbols (see the 'Supporting children' section on pages 142-7) can be used to support the existing communication of children with speech and language or hearing difficulties.

Encourage children speaking languages other than English to use gestures and actions to support their communication skills. Value and welcome their contributions in their home language as well as attempts at new words and vocabulary.

Challenge some children to work in pairs using talk to cooperate, organize and clarify their ideas.

Learning steps
- Use action, sometimes with limited talk, that is largely connected with the here and now.
- Use language as a means of widening contacts, and sharing feelings, experiences and thoughts.
- Talk activities through, reflecting on and modifying what the children are doing.
- Use language to imagine and recreate roles and experiences.
- Use talk to organize sequence and clarify ideas, feelings and events.

Look, listen and note
How do they:
- show that they understand?
- use language (including signs, symbols and gestures) in pretend and imaginary play?
- (for children speaking languages others than English) develop and use their dominant language, as well as gesture and intonation to convey meaning?

How do they…? – this section is developed from the 'Look, listen and note' section of the EYFS and guides practitioners, parents and carers to assess the child's development which will inform the next steps of learning.

Animals

This chapter offers plenty of opportunities for imaginative play and learning. We practise our animal communication skills through jungle jingles, listening and lotto games. We follow animal tracks when exploring the classroom and create our own animal prints, tactile books and fantasy creatures. There is a fishy phonics game, animal snap and enchanting rhymes and stories to entice all learners.

Chapter contents

Role-play area ideas

The following role-play areas will provide a fun and meaningful learning context for all learners:

- zoo
- vets
- pet shop
- farm
- jungle
- African safari
- garden.

Songs and rhymes

These song and rhyme suggestions can be adapted by adding alternative animals and using children's names to add interest:

- 'Five little speckled frogs'
- 'Daddy's taking us to the zoo tomorrow'
- 'Old MacDonald had a farm'
- 'Five little ducks went swimming one day'
- 'How much is that doggy in the window?'
- 'Pussy cat, pussy cat'
- 'Mary had a little lamb'
- 'Little Bo Peep'
- 'Flutter, flutter butterfly'.

Hands-on learning

Real-life encounters with animals provide exciting, meaningful and concrete experiences to support the understanding of all children. A class pet or a visit to a farm or zoo provides great motivation for future learning.

Parents as partners home activities

Ask parents and carers to send in pictures of family pets. These can be shared with other children during circle time and in communication, language and literacy activities.

Invite parents and carers who are using alternative languages, such as signing and language, other than English, to come into school to share animal stories, rhymes and songs in their mother tongue, or teach children animal signs and symbols. Ask parents and carers what noises they use to represent different animals, for example do they say 'neigh' for a horse?

Links with the Early Learning Goals and EYFS

Personal, emotional and social development:

- Be confident to try new activities, initiate ideas and communicate in a familiar group.

Knowledge and understanding:

- Investigate objects and materials by using all of their senses as appropriate.
- Find out about and investigate some features of living things.

Creative development:

- Express and communicate their ideas, thoughts and feelings by using a widening range of materials, suitable tools, imaginative role play, movement, and designing and making and a variety of songs and musical instruments.

- Use their imagination in role play and stories.

ACTIVITY 1
Crazy creatures

You will need

Pictures of animals, soft toy/model animals, a clear safe space with a PE mat, an animal adventure story book such as *Walking Through the Jungle* by Julie Lacome (Walker Books).

Online resources available

Vocabulary
move, copy, listen, animal, creature, small, big, slow, fast

Show the children pictures and models of different creatures or animals. Talk about the animals and encourage the children to think about how they move and sound.

Next put the children into pairs and ask them to think of an animal they would like to be. Encourage them to think about how the animal moves and sounds by talking through their ideas with their partner.

Use a suitable story, such as *Walking Through the Jungle*, or create an imaginative story about a nature walk as this could incorporate a wider variety of animals. As you tell the story ask the children to listen for their animal to be mentioned. Encourage the children to respond in turn using their chosen animal movements and sounds.

Meeting different learners' needs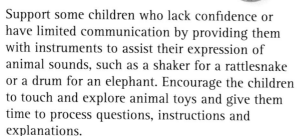

Support some children who lack confidence or have limited communication by providing them with instruments to assist their expression of animal sounds, such as a shaker for a rattlesnake or a drum for an elephant. Encourage the children to touch and explore animal toys and give them time to process questions, instructions and explanations.

Provide a safe space on a PE mat for a small group of children to work alongside children with a physical impairment. Encourage them to explore movements in a lying or sitting position.

Encourage and value children with EAL to use their home language to talk about animals and use a range of gestures, actions and intonation to convey meaning.

Challenge some children to create their own imaginative story about a nature walk.

Learning steps
- Take pleasure in making and listening to a wide variety of sounds.
- Listen to others in a one-to-one situation or small groups when the conversation interests them.
- Respond to simple instructions.
- Enjoy listening to and using spoken language, and readily turn to it in their play and learning.

Look, listen and note
How do they:
- communicate in different ways?
- demonstrate their understanding of the instructions they are given?
- communicate with others?

ACTIVITY 2
Animal footsteps

Vocabulary
print, hold, draw, trace, copy

You will need
Objects for printing such as sponges, blocks or footprint stamps, three or four sets of animal footprints of varying detail, colour and size, animal soft toys, paper, paints, flat shallow painting trays, paint brushes.
Online resources available

Invite the children into a classroom that displays tracks of different animal footprints. Explain that they will be explorers looking for hidden animals. Show them an example animal that they will be looking for, to support all children's understanding of the task. Encourage the children to work in groups to follow the different tracks and find animals hidden around the room.

When the children reach the animal, ask them to compare and trace the different footprints. Encourage them to discuss differences in size, form and shape. Ask the children to make their own animal footprints by printing or painting using the various tools and resources.

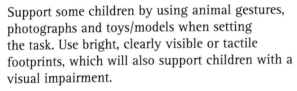

Meeting different learners' needs

Support some children by using animal gestures, photographs and toys/models when setting the task. Use bright, clearly visible or tactile footprints, which will also support children with a visual impairment.

For children learning EAL, pair them with other children who can guide them in this task.

Challenge some children to paint more complex footprints using a brush with control and precision.

Learning steps
- Make random marks using their fingers and some tools.
- Use one-handed tools and equipment.
- Draw lines and circles using gross motor movements.
- Begin to show some control when using tools and equipment.

Look, listen and note
How do they:
- make marks in different ways?
- hold the print-/mark-making tools in their hands?
- control the print-/mark-making tools?

Let's All Play

ACTIVITY 3
The Three Billy Goats Gruff

You will need
The book *The Three Billy Goats Gruff* (Ladybird) along with the following props: a water tray, large pebbles/stones, a piece of wood for the bridge, a troll (this could be made from play-dough or plasticine), three toy goats of different sizes.

Vocabulary
goats, troll, bridge, river, beginning, middle, end

Introduce the characters using the toy goats and troll. Read the story *The Three Billy Goats Gruff* with a small group of children and encourage them to join in with the repeated refrains used in book. Draw their attention to the pictures and encourage them to talk about what they can see.

Ask the children to help you create a story set for the book using a water tray, stones and a wooden bridge. Encourage them to take on different characters and retell the story using the story scene and models, for example hiding the troll under the bridge and deepening their voice to say, 'Who's that going over my bridge?'

Meeting different learners' needs

Support some children by asking them to act out the story using the props rather than focusing on their verbal contributions.

For children learning EAL repeat the story over several sessions and use a dual-language book where possible.

Challenge some children to adopt the language pattern of the story, use different voices for the characters and talk about the sequence of events.

Learning steps
- Listen to and join in with stories and poems, one-to-one and also in small groups.
- Retell narratives in the correct sequence, drawing on language patterns of *stories*.
- Show an understanding of the elements of stories, such as the main character, sequence of events and openings, and how information can be found in non-fiction texts to answer questions about where, who, why and how.

Look, listen and note
How do they:
- show they understand and retell the story using actions, words and phrases?
- demonstrate that they understand the main elements of the story, using phrases such as 'In the beginning' and 'The end'?

ACTIVITY 4
Fishy phonics

Vocabulary
letter, sound, listen, spell, read, word

You will need
Laminated pictures of sea creatures which display different lower-case letters with paper clips attached, magnetic fishing rods, water play trays, plastic letters.

Online resources available

Put the sea creatures in a water-tray and ask the children to see what letters they can 'catch' using their fishing rod. Ask the children to name each letter and give its sound by prompting them with questions such as 'What letter have you caught?' Encourage some children to create sound blends using two letters such as 'sh' or 'th', or show them how to arrange the lettered creatures to make simple regular words for example, 'm – a – t'.

Meeting different learners' needs

Support some children by focusing on listening, enjoying and creating different sounds to represent the water and creatures, for example 'splish', 'splash', 'plop'. Add glitter to the water to add interest for children reluctant to engage in the activity. Also encourage the children to feel the shape of the plastic letters to support their understanding.

Model the letter sounds for children learning EAL and encourage them to echo these.

Challenge some children to create phonetically

Learning steps
- Show an interest in play with sounds.
- Distinguish one sound from another.
- Link sounds to letters, naming and sounding the letters of the alphabet.
- Use their phonic knowledge to write simple regular words and make phonetically plausible attempts at more complex words.

Look, listen and note
How do they:
- use emerging communication methods and languages they understand to support their learning?
- distinguish between the differences in vocal sounds?
- link sounds to letters?
- use blending and segmenting, and, using grapheme-phoneme knowledge, spell simple words?

ACTIVITY 5
Animal sound lotto

You will need
Commercially produced sound lotto game or recorded animal sounds with matching animal photographs.
Online resources available

Vocabulary
listen, same, copy, different, animal

This activity works best with a small group and minimal background noise to support the listening skills of all learners. Demonstrate how to play the game by playing an animal sound effect and finding the matching animal photograph/ model.

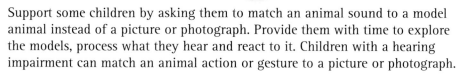

Meeting different learners' needs

Support some children by asking them to match an animal sound to a model animal instead of a picture or photograph. Provide them with time to explore the models, process what they hear and react to it. Children with a hearing impairment can match an animal action or gesture to a picture or photograph.

For children learning EAL, provide them with time to observe the game before joining in.

Challenge some children who are learning their letter sounds to find the initial letter sound of an animal, for example 's' for snake or 'sh' for sheep.

Learning steps
- Frequently repeat words or signs that they hear or see, with one or more keywords repeated.
- Distinguish one sound from another.
- Show an interest in play with letters and sounds.

Look, listen and note
How do they:
- build their vocabulary of words and signs?
- listen and respond to different sounds?
- demonstrate an understanding of matching different sounds to pictures or objects?

ACTIVITY 6
Feely books

Vocabulary
touch, texture, feel, write, word, sentence

You will need
Photographs/pictures of animals, examples of touch and feel books, glue sticks, blank pages/books, a variety of textured materials, feely bags.

Online resources available

Hide different textured materials in feely bags.

Encourage the children to feel and describe the different textures. Ask the children to think about different animals and how they feel. Match texture samples to animal pictures or models, for example a piece of soft fur to a cat or a piece of leather to an elephant.

Show the children examples of different texture books and encourage them to explore the textures for themselves. Explain that they will work in small groups/pairs to make their own animal feely book. Ask the children to choose an animal picture/photograph and select a texture sample to add to the page. Model writing a sentence about each animal, for example: 'The cat is soft.' Ensure that all children have an opportunity to create a page when working in a group.

Meeting different learners' needs

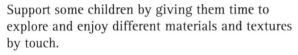

Support some children by giving them time to explore and enjoy different materials and textures by touch.

For children learning EAL, ensure that they have an opportunity to explore children's books displaying a variety of scripts to support language awareness.

Challenge some children to form simple words and sentences to record their ideas using capital letters and full stops.

Learning steps
- Grasp and manipulate different textures.
- Examine the writing that others make.
- Use writing as a means of recording and communicating.
- Attempt writing for different purposes.
- Write simple sentences, sometimes using punctuation.

Look, listen and note
How do they:
- demonstrate an interest in the marks they make?
- talk about the pages they have made?
- recognize writing on a page?

Sheep

ACTIVITY 7
Jungle jingle

You will need
Photographs/pictures of animals, animal models/toys.
Online resources available

Vocabulary
listen, rhythm, sound, sing, song

Display between three to six familiar jungle animals. Name each animal and demonstrate the sound that each animal makes, for example a parrot that squawks or a lion that roars.

Explain that the children are going to make up their own jungle jingle. Start the song by singing the first verse (an example is given below). Encourage the children to come up with further verses of the jingle by choosing animals and sounds of their own.

(Sing to the tune of 'Old MacDonald had a farm'.)
'In the jungle hear the sounds
ee i ee i o
And in the jungle lives a snake
ee i ee i o
With a s-s-s here and a s-s-s there ...'

Learning steps
- Join in with repeated refrains and anticipate phrases in rhymes/songs.
- Listen to songs with increasing attention and recall.
- Consistently develop a simple song.
- Listen with enjoyment to songs, music and rhymes and make up their own song within a group.

Look, listen and note
How do they:
- act out the rhyme/song?
- demonstrate an awareness of turn taking?
- make up songs and remember rhymes off by heart?

Meeting different learners' needs

Support some children with communication difficulties to use a big Mack (see the 'Supporting children' section on pages 142–7) or an animal toy with a sound effect for them to activate when it is their turn.

Encourage children with EAL to use their home language to talk about animals. Welcome their non-verbal contributions to the activity such as animal gestures and actions.

Challenge some children to make up their own animal jingle to a different tune such as 'Twinkle, twinkle little star' or 'Row, row, row your boat'.

ACTIVITY 8
A trip to the pet shop

Vocabulary
animal, visit, food, water, bedding, bowl, brush, treat, list, write

You will need
A classroom pet or an animal on loan to the class for a week, relevant items that are needed to take care of the pet such as, food, bedding, water bottle, cleaning equipment and a cage.

You will also need
Pet information leaflets, books, posters and pictures, strips of paper for lists, pens, pencils, crayons and a noticeboard.

Online resources available

Introduce the animal and ask the children to talk quietly, reminding them that animals may be easily frightened. Explain that the animal relies on us to take care of it and we need to go to a shop to buy some of the things it needs. Discuss what these items are, where we would buy them and why it needs them.

Look at posters, leaflets, books and pictures containing information about caring for animals. Model to the children how to write a list to plan what they will need to buy from the shop. Help them to create their own lists using words, small pictures or symbols.

Once the children have been to the shop (this can be a role-play shop or a visit to a real pet shop) explore the items using all of their senses, for example smelling the food, feeling the water and listening to the rustling bedding.

Meeting different learners' needs

As this is a multi-sensory activity it is particularly effective for supporting different learners' needs. Provide children with the opportunity to add their own 'writing' to the list. This may be simple mark-making which they ascribe meaning to.

For children learning EAL, focus on the use of pictures when creating their list using keywords and simple gestures to support their understanding of the different items and what they are used for.

Challenge some children to write their own list, adopting a bullet point or numbered format to structure their writing.

Learning steps

- Ascribe meaning to marks that they see in different places.
- Begin to break the flow of speech into words.
- Attempt writing for different purposes, using features of different forms such as lists.
- Use phonic knowledge to attempt to write words.

Look, listen and note
How do they:

- demonstrate an interest in the marks they make?
- use writing to record and communicate?
- use phonic knowledge to attempt to write words?

ACTIVITY 9
Wiggly worms

Vocabulary
copy, print, draw, write, straight, wiggly, curved

You will need
Pictures of worms or real worms, string cut into different lengths, aprons, paper, brown paints, paint trays and pipe cleaners.

Online resources available

Introduce the pictures or observe real worms.
Invite the children to hold, touch and describe the worms, washing their hands immediately afterwards. Discuss the different types of lines and shapes the worms create with their bodies.

Ask the children to use, bend and mould pipe cleaners to create different worm shapes. Invite the children to trace and feel each other's different pipe-cleaner worms and describe them using descriptive words such as straight, curved and wiggly.

Encourage the children to use their index fingers to dip into the paint and make worm shapes on the paper. Some children can dip string into the paint and arrange it on the paper to create worm prints.

Meeting different learners' needs

Support some children by encouraging them to explore the paint and textures using their hands and guide their finger to make wiggly lines. Use bright, large, clearly visible pipe cleaners against a contrasting background to support children with a visual impairment.

Support children learning EAL by finding out some keywords such as 'write', 'look' and 'copy' in their home language and use these when appropriate to support their understanding.

Challenge some children to paint worms in the shape of letters, for example s, l and c, with control and precision.

Learning steps
- Make random marks using their fingers and some tools.
- Draw lines and circles using gross motor movements.
- Manipulate objects with increasing control.
- Form recognizable letters.

Look, listen and note
How do they:
- make marks in different ways?
- hold and control the print/mark-making tools in their hand?

ACTIVITY 10
A visit to the vet's

Vocabulary
medicine, feed, drink, injection, bandage, ill, healthy

You will need
A vet's role-play area including vets' instruments and equipment such as bandages, syringes, white overall and a thermometer.

You will also need
Leaflets, posters and notices, a waiting-room area, soft pet toys, magazines for the waiting room, a reception desk and equipment.

Introduce the vet's role-play area to the children by demonstrating actions, language and gestures or by using a video of a vet programme. Ask the children What do vets do? How do they cure sick animals? Who has been to a vet's? Encourage the children to share pictures of their animals from home and share their personal experiences.

Encourage the children to take on different roles and act out imaginary scenarios in character. Then encourage them to talk about what is happening.

Meeting different learners' needs

Support some children by using photographs of animals and by encouraging them to engage in symbolic play, for example stroking the toy animals. Voice output devices and symbols (see the 'Supporting children' section on pages 142–7) can be used to support the existing communication of children with communication difficulties.

For children learning EAL use gestures and actions to support their communication skills. Value and welcome their contributions in their home language as well as attempts at new words and vocabulary.

Challenge some children to work in pairs, use talk to cooperate, organize and clarify their ideas.

Learning steps

- Use actions, sometimes supported by limited talk, that are largely connected with the here and now.
- Use language as a means of widening contacts, and sharing feelings, experiences and thoughts.
- Talk activities through, reflecting on and modifying what they are doing.
- Use language to imagine and recreate roles and experiences.
- Use talk to organize sequence and clarify thinking ideas, feelings and events.

Look, listen and note
How do they:

- show that they understand?
- use language (including signs, symbols and gestures) in pretend and imaginary play?
- (for children speaking languages other than English) develop and use their dominant language, as well as their use of gesture and intonation to convey meaning?

ACTIVITY 11
Very hungry children!

Vocabulary
caterpillar, butterfly, pretend, beginning, middle, end, next

You will need
The Very Hungry Caterpillar by Eric Carle (Hamish Hamilton) along with the following props: caterpillar/sock puppet, a butterfly picture/model, large green paper/real leaf with a small cotton ball attached, real food or play food from the story, press light switch (to represent the sun).

Online resources available

In small groups read the story of *The Very Hungry Caterpillar* drawing attention to the repetitive language and encourage the children to join in with repeated refrains.

Invite the children to retell the story by acting out the events in sequence, using the visual cues and story props. Encourage them to use language to sequence events such as, 'beginning' and 'next'.

Meeting different learners' needs

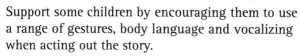

Support some children by encouraging them to use a range of gestures, body language and vocalizing when acting out the story.

For children learning EAL, use dual-language books or invite parents and carers or qualified bilingual adults to read the story in the language used at home.

Challenge some children to sound out and read unfamiliar words using their knowledge of phonics.

Learning steps
- Show some interest in stories, songs and rhymes.
- Listen and join in with stories and poems, one-to-one and also in small groups.
- Begin to be aware of the ways stories are structured.
- Retell narratives in the correct sequence, drawing on language patterns of the stories.
- Show some understanding of the main elements of the story, such as the main character, sequence of events and openings.

Look, listen and note
How do they:
- use talk and actions to retell the story?
- remember the sequence of the story?

ACTIVITY 12
Beautiful butterflies

Vocabulary
wings, body, antenna, caterpillar, butterfly

You will need
Various cardboard boxes and tubes, pipe cleaners, various coloured paper/tissue paper/polyethylene, glitter, sequins, glue, scissors and photographs/pictures of butterflies.

Online resources available

Read or recap the story *The Very Hungry Caterpillar* drawing attention to the changes that took place as the caterpillar became a beautiful butterfly. Ask the children how the little caterpillar might have felt as he woke to find he had become a brightly coloured butterfly. Encourage the children to share their feelings and thoughts and welcome different ideas and opinions.

Explain that the children are going to make butterflies using various materials. Label the different parts of the butterfly to introduce new words and vocabulary, for example 'Here are the butterfly's antenna'.

Ask the children to talk through how they are going to create their own butterfly from the materials provided. Encourage them to talk about what they are doing. Ensure that you welcome ideas from different children.

Meeting different learners' needs

Support some children by focusing on simple vocabulary, such as butterfly and caterpillar, and naming colours. Use simple emotions puppets to support the expression and understanding of emotions and ideas for some children.

Encourage children learning EAL to use gestures and actions to support their communication skills. Value and welcome their contributions in their home language as well as attempts at new words and vocabulary.

Challenge some children to work in pairs, use talk to cooperate, organize and clarify their ideas.

Learning steps
- Use action, sometimes with limited talk, that is largely connected with the here and now.
- Use language as a means of widening contacts by sharing feelings, experiences and thoughts.
- Talk activities through, reflecting on and modifying what they are doing.
- Use language to imagine and recreate roles and experiences.
- Use talk to organize sequence and clarify thinking ideas, feelings and events.

Look, listen and note
How do they:
- show that they understand?
- use language (including signs, symbols and gestures) in pretend and imaginary play?
- (for children speaking languages others than English) develop and use their dominant language, as well as gesture and intonation to convey meaning?

Food glorious food!

This chapter offers plenty of opportunities for multi-sensory learning and finding out about food in different cultures and countries. We tantalize our taste buds with tasty alphabet books, silly shopping lists, delicious porridge recipes, scrumptious biscuits and tempting traditional tales. Writing becomes fun and mouth-wateringly messy when practising forming letters using different materials. Finally, we have lots of noisy fun in the kitchen.

Chapter contents

Role-play area ideas

These role-play areas will provide a fun and meaningful learning context for all learners:

- supermarket
- café
- fish and chip shop
- greengrocer
- bakery
- ice-cream van
- restaurant.

Songs and rhymes

These song suggestions can be adapted by adding examples of food from different cultures and places, and from children's own ideas to add interest and relevance:

- 'Let's bake a cake'
- 'Five current buns in a baker's shop'
- 'Hot cross buns'
- 'Jelly on a plate'
- 'Pat a cake'
- 'Oranges and lemons'
- 'Sing a song of sixpence'
- 'Ten fat sausages sizzling in a pan'.

Hands-on learning

Hands-on activities with real food provide excellent multi-sensory learning opportunities which can be a great motivator for all children. Provide children with opportunities to explore a range of food and use this motivating topic to promote healthy living and a good diet. Ensure that the children have the opportunity to be involved with food preparation, cooking and baking, with a focus on hygiene and the importance of keeping healthy and safe.

Parents as partners home activities

Ask parents and carers to send examples of food packaging from their homes. These can be added to the shop role play. Encourage a variety of different types of food from different cultural backgrounds that display different types of food, print and languages.

Invite parents and carers into school to share their favourite home recipes with the children during cookery classes or tasting sessions. Support the children to have an awareness of and interest in cultural differences linked to food.

Links with the Early Learning Goals and EYFS

Personal, emotional and social development:

- Have a developing respect for their own cultures and beliefs, and those of other people.
- Understand that people have different needs, views, cultures and beliefs that need to be treated with respect.
- Understand that they can expect others to treat their needs, views, cultures and beliefs with respect.

Knowledge and understanding of the world:

- Investigate objects and materials by using all of their senses as appropriate.

Physical development:

- Recognize the importance of keeping healthy and the things which contribute to this.

Creative development:

- Respond in a variety of ways to what they see, hear, smell, touch and feel.
- Express and communicate their ideas, thoughts and feelings by using a widening range of materials, suitable tools, imaginative role play, movement, designing and making and a variety of songs and musical instruments.
- Use their imagination in role play and stories.

ACTIVITY 13
Silly spaghetti

You will need
Cooked soft spaghetti,
uncooked spaghetti,
examples of shapes, lines and letters,
shallow trays and blindfolds.
Online resources available

Vocabulary
straight, curved, round, zigzag, shape,
up, down

Introduce cooked and uncooked pasta to the group using a blindfold game. Encourage the children to touch, feel and compare the two by describing them, focusing on adjectives which describe shape, form and texture.

Remove the blindfolds and ask the children to create simple shapes, line patterns and letters in trays using the two forms of pasta. Encourage them to recognize the suitability of different types of pasta for creating different lines and shapes. For example, 'Can you make a circle using uncooked pasta? Why not?' Support the children to use a combination of cooked and uncooked pasta to create letters, focusing on straight, curved or zigzag lines. Use shapes and directional language whilst encouraging them to feel and form letters correctly.

Meeting different learners' needs

Support some children who are not able to form letters to explore the different forms and textures of pasta and develop their hand–eye coordination, manipulative and fine motor skills. Provide a blackboard (this could be made from a laminated piece of A4 paper) for children with a visual impairment to work on, to give better contrast.

Provide children learning EAL with clear visual cues to support their understanding. Provide them with examples of shapes, various line patterns and letters to feel, copy and trace.

Challenge some children to create simple short words such as 'at', 'it' or 'cat'.

Learning steps
- Manipulate and explore the pasta.
- Draw lines and circles using gross motor movements.
- Manipulate objects with increasing control.
- Begin to form recognizable letters.

Look, listen and note
How do they:
- develop and use fine motor skills?
- control materials to create different lines, shapes and letters?
- attempt to produce recognizable letters?

ACTIVITY 14
Lassi begins with 'L'

Vocabulary
trace, copy, letter, write, draw

You will need

Several different items of food packaging which clearly display the product name in lower-case letters (some popular supermarket chains produce economy brands with lower-case text and labels), shallow trays, letter flash cards, plastic letters, hand wash resources and aprons!

Online resources available

Display a shopping bag containing various food items in their original packaging. Select different children to take an item from the bag. Encourage them to explore and name the product using picture cues, text on labels and packaging, as well as using all senses as appropriate.

Ask the children to help with filling shallow trays with different foods taken from the shopping bag. Demonstrate to the children how to trace the plastic letters and copy lines, shapes and letters in the different materials using their fingers and hands. Encourage the children to practise writing an initial letter sound in a chosen resource. For examples 't' in tea leaves, 's' in salt and 'j' in jam.

Meeting different learners' needs

Support some children to make marks in the different materials and explore using all their senses. Use labels displaying clear large bold text and provide a magnifying glass or low-vision aid (see 'Further reading and information' section on pages 142–7) to support children with a visual impairment when reading text on food packaging.

Provide children learning EAL with clear visual cues, with examples of letters and words to support their understanding. Include food items relevant to different cultures and provide examples of food packaging in different languages.

Challenge some children to create letter blends such as, 'sh' in sherbet or to write phonetically plausible attempts at words beginning with an initial letter sound, for example 'tee' in tea leaves.

Learning steps

- Make random marks with their fingers.
- Draw lines and circles using gross motor movements.
- Begin to use anticlockwise movements and retrace vertical lines.
- Begin to form recognizable letters.

Look, listen and note
How do they:

- make various marks?
- control materials to create different lines, shapes and letters?
- attempt to produce recognizable letters?

ACTIVITY 15
Keeping safe!

Vocabulary
danger, safe, not safe, clean, sharp, hot, electric, water, list

Explain that you want the children to create a list of rules for keeping safe in the kitchen. Explain what is meant by rules, using a familiar example such as the class rules. Use photographs or role-play equipment and where possible visit the kitchen area. Identify the different hazards in the kitchen, for example a hot oven, a kettle, sharp utensils or the sound of a smoke detector.

Use photographs and objects to prompt the children's memory and aid their understanding of the task. Ask them to take turns in identifying and discussing potential hazards. With children's contributions, scribe a list of safety rules from their findings. Ask the children to think about additional hazards that cannot always be seen, such as dirty hands, or ensuring cultural food laws are kept, for example keeping meat away from dairy products in some kitchens.

Meeting different learners' needs

Support some children by using visual cues such as a familiar danger sign displayed around the school or centre. You can also add pictures or symbols (see the 'Supporting children' section on pages 142–7) to the text you scribe, to support their understanding of the written text.

Encourage children learning EAL to share cultural practices from their home and use visual cues to support their understanding of danger and keeping safe.

Challenge some children to design a danger logo with a short caption to warn of hazards in the kitchen.

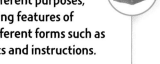

Learning steps
- Examine the writing of an adult.
- Ascribe meaning to writing.
- Use writing as a means of recording and communicating.
- Attempt writing for different purposes, using features of different forms such as lists and instructions.

Look, listen and note
How do they:
- demonstrate their understanding of recording using a list?
- give meaning to the marks they make?
- use writing to record things or to communicate?
- use writing for different purposes?

ACTIVITY 16
Tasty alphabet books!

Vocabulary
letter, page, book, write, sentence, food, picture, alphabet

You will need
Examples of alphabet books (books which provide examples of objects beginning with each letter of the alphabet), blank books (text can be added beforehand to save time during the activity), glue sticks, scissors and pencils.

You will also need
Various examples of real food, each beginning with a different letter of the alphabet. Assign a different letter to each child in your class and ask him or her to bring in an item of food beginning with that letter sound. Provide each child with a list of possibilities and ask him or her to bring in food from home. Avoid examples with a difficult initial sound beginning such as sugar and remember to check for children's allergies. Take and print photographs of the food brought in prior to starting the session and ensure that you have a different food example for each letter of the alphabet.

Online resources available

Show the children examples of alphabet books and invite them to help 'read' the book focusing on the connection between the letter and the initial sound of the item in the picture. For example, 'a is for apple'.

Invite the children to explore various food items by using all their senses as appropriate, including taste, smell and by exploring the shape and texture of different foods. Encourage them to name food items in photographs and give their initial letter sound, including those from different cultures and religions, for example 'b is for bhaji'.

Write one sentence for each page, for example 'a is for apple' and 's is for sandwich'. Encourage them to think of their favourite food from home. Invite each child to contribute to a single page by adding a suitable picture or drawing and supporting him or her to add a letter or word. Encourage the groups to read each other's alphabet books.

Meeting different learners' needs

Support some children by encouraging them to explore the food using all of their senses. If some children find it difficult to record their ideas using drawings or words, they may use pictures or symbols (see the 'Supporting children' section on pages 142–7). Add sand/glitter to the letters to create texture letters that help children to 'feel' the letters, and use Braille aids where appropriate (see the 'Further reading and information' section on pages 148–9). Praise children for adding their 'writing', which can be random mark making, to their page in the book.

Incorporate food which reflects cultural diversity and take care to pronounce the names of different food items correctly. Provide children learning EAL with a variety of different scripts displayed on food packaging, some of which may be more familiar to them, to support their understanding of different forms of writing for the same purpose.

Challenge some children to write short sentences using simple punctuation and phonetically plausible attempts at unfamiliar words.

Learning steps
- Examine the marks they and others make.
- Sometimes give meaning to marks as they draw.
- Break the flow of speech into words.
- Use writing as a means of recording and communicating.
- Attempt to write for different purposes using features of different forms such as sentences to record factual information.
- Write labels, captions and begin to form simple sentences, sometimes using punctuation.

Look, listen and note
How do they:
- talk about the marks they have made?
- demonstrate their understanding of recording by using words and pictures?
- make use of phonic knowledge as they attempt to write words and simple sentences?

ACTIVITY 17
Bish, bash, bosh!

You will need

Pairs of kitchen items to be used as music makers such as two plastic jugs, two pans, two pots or two metal bowls.

You will also need

A collection of beaters such as wooden spoons.

Vocabulary
rhythm, listen, repeat, same, sound, loud, quiet

Demonstrate to the children how the pots and pans make different sounds when hit with a wooden spoon. Also show them that identical items make the same sounds when hit with the spoon.

Share out one set of pots and pans and so on among the children and ask them to play their item when they see and hear you playing its matching item, for example you hit a plastic jug and the child with the matching plastic jug copies you. Encourage the children to describe the sound and identify it.

Then ask the children to turn so they are facing away from you. Repeat the activity asking the children to listen for their matching item being played and encouraging them to play theirs in response. Finally, let some of the children have a turn in leading the game by making different sounds.

Meeting different learners' needs

Support some children to explore creating different sounds by tapping or stroking using their hands, body or different beaters, for example beaters made of wood, plastic or metal.

Support the understanding and involvement of children learning EAL or a hearing impairment by asking them not to turn away but to keep their eyes on you. Support them to find the same item by matching the sound makers visually as well as by their sound.

To make the game more difficult ask the children to copy different rhythms and follow different sound patterns, for example pan-pot-jug, pan-pot-jug and so on.

Learning steps
- Increasingly using sounds and words to represent objects around them.
- Distinguish one sound from another.
- Show an interest in playing with sounds.
- Enjoy rhythmic activities.

Look, listen and note
How do they:
- discriminate between sounds?
- remember and repeat a sound or rhythm?

ACTIVITY 18
Silly sounding shopping list

Vocabulary
list, listen, sound, beginning, letter, word

You will need
A whiteboard and pens, posters, books, food photographs and pictures from magazines, examples of different menus displaying pictures of food, plastic/texture letters.

Online resources available

Share the appetizing pictures of food with the children and discuss which are their favourites. Focus on the initial letter sound of an item of food by sounding it out and writing it on a whiteboard. Demonstrate to the children how to generate a string of descriptive words beginning with the same sound, for example fried fish fingers, pickled peppers, juicy jam or soggy sandwiches.

Invite the children to think of an item of food and support them to generate a string of words with the same sound. Scribe their ideas to create a silly sounding shopping list. Use photographs, menus, books and posters to prompt them to include a range of multi-cultural foods.

Meeting different learners' needs

Support some children by asking them to make choices using real food and select pictures to show what they would like to add to the shopping list. Encourage children to feel the shape of different plastic/texture letters.

Encourage children learning EAL to echo sounds and words being aware that not all foods may be familiar to them.

Challenge some children to string up to five words together in a descriptive alliteration phrase.

Learning steps

- Increasingly experiment with using sounds, words, signs and symbols to represent objects around them.
- Distinguish one sound from another.
- Show interest in play with sounds.
- Show an awareness of alliteration.
- Hear and say sounds in words in the order in which they occur.

Look, listen and note
How do they:

- listen to and recognize different sounds?
- know and use some letter sounds?
- demonstrate an understanding of the initial sound in a word?

ACTIVITY 19
A tempting traditional tale

Vocabulary
story, repeat, character, beginning, middle, end, next, sentence, word

You will need
The book, *The Gingerbread Man*, based on a traditional tale, by Anja Rieger (Ladybird), along with the following props: a rolling pin, boards, aprons, play-dough, role-play oven, a man-shaped biscuit cutter, toy fox, piece of blue material (to represent the river), a water jug, shallow tray, fresh ginger biscuits to taste (remember to check that no children have allergies to any ingredients in the biscuits used).

You will also need
Pictures or models of the characters in the story.

Online resources available

Read the book, *The Gingerbread Man*, several times with the children, using the props and actions. Once they are familiar with the sequence of events, the language pattern within the story and main characters, explain that they will be helping to make a large display about the book.

Explain to the children that they are going to be thinking about the sequence of the story by ordering the events that take place. Ask the children to work in pairs to create various stages of the story. They can be set different tasks according to their ability. For example, two younger children can make gingerbread biscuits using play-dough and a role-play oven to represent the beginning of the story. Two other children, who have difficulties writing, can select pictures and glue them onto a background to recreate other scenes from the story. Meanwhile some older children can draw characters and events adding captions and labels.

Create a display using the children's contributions and use it to discuss the order in which events take place, ultimately encouraging them to retell the story in their own words. As the children suggest their ideas, the teacher can scribe these to add to the display.

Meeting different learners' needs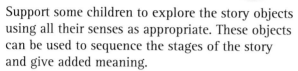

Support some children to explore the story objects using all their senses as appropriate. These objects can be used to sequence the stages of the story and give added meaning.

Remember that while many children will be familiar with the story of *The Gingerbread Man*, it will be new to others, including those learning EAL. Repeat the book over several sessions and use dual-language books where appropriate, that can also be sent home as reading books.

Challenge some children to sequence a complex string of events including discussing how the characters might have felt throughout the story. Ask them to recall the story by themselves and where appropriate make their own book to retell the story.

Learning steps
- Listen and join in with stories in one-one and also in small groups.
- Begin to be aware of the way stories are structured.
- Retell narratives in the correct sequence, drawing on the language patterns of the story.
- Show an understanding of the main elements of the story, such as main character, sequence of events and openings.

Look, listen and note
How do they:
- respond to the objects, pictures and story?
- retell a story, using words and phrases from the original story, *The Gingerbread Man*?

ACTIVITY 20
Three hungry bears

Vocabulary
listen, instruction, remember, describe, taste

You will need
The book, *Goldilocks and the Three Bears* (Ladybird), porridge oats, containers of various shapes and sizes, spoons of various sizes and made from different materials, salt, honey, jam, water jug, three toy bears and aprons.

Online resources available

Read the book, *Goldilocks and the Three Bears*, with the children. Talk about the three bears and explain that the children will be helping to make porridge for them by following instructions.

Explore the ingredients using all the senses and introduce new adjectives to describe the different tastes and ingredients, for example 'scrumptiously sweet honey'. Model appropriate language used to negotiate and plan the activity with the children. For example, 'Would it be right to add salt to make this porridge taste sweet?'

Give pairs of children different instructions to follow to make porridge for the three bears. For example, 'Can Isaan and Claire make sweet porridge for mummy bear please?' Encourage the children to develop their language and memory skills during play through discussion and collaboration with their peers.

Meeting different learners' needs

Support some children by encouraging them to share their likes and dislikes during tasting activities. Ensure that children with communication difficulties have access to signs/symbols and other visual cues to support their understanding of the activity and to help them to express themselves. Also use simple instructions, for example 'Can you make some porridge for baby bear please?'

For children learning EAL, value non-verbal communication such as gestures and attempts to join in using their home language. Respond by using additional words, gestures, objects and other visual cues to support two-way understanding.

Challenge some children by adding adjectives and keywords to create more complex requests such as, 'Can you make some salty porridge in a large round bowl with a wooden spoon for daddy bear please?'

Learning steps

- Understand simple sentences.
- Respond to simple instructions.
- Use vocabulary and forms of speech that are increasingly influenced by their experience of books.
- Enjoy listening to and using spoken and written language, and readily turn to it in their play and learning.
- Sustain attentive listening, responding to what they have heard with relevant comments, questions or actions.

Look, listen and note
How do they:

- show their understanding of instructions?
- use and develop their preferred language (such as sign or foreign languages)?
- concentrate on what others say and their responses to what they have heard?

ACTIVITY 21
Where does this go?

Vocabulary
dairy, meat, fish, vegetables, fruit, fridge, cupboard, pantry, freezer, grains and cereals

You will need
A shopping bag full of groceries including dairy products, meat, wheat and grain, fruit and vegetables, and sugar products (you can ask the children to bring in different items from home to cut down on cost), and a home role-play area.

Introduce a shopping bag full of groceries. Explore the items inside with the children and encourage them to share their experiences of going to the shops or helping parents/carers to pack their shopping away. Explain and describe unfamiliar words to the children such as 'dairy', 'grains and cereals' and 'pantry'.

Let them take turns to pretend to be in their house and to put an item away in the role-play home area. Extend their use of language to explain why and where things are put in the kitchen. For example, put milk in the fridge to prevent it going off quickly. Support the children to extend their vocabulary to classify, group and name items in their play.

Meeting different learners' needs

Support some children by encouraging them to touch and explore the real-food items and give them time to process questions, instructions and explanations.

Ensure that the children have opportunities to share cultural practices from their home relating to food laws such as keeping meat separate from dairy products in some kitchens. Also, where appropriate, for children learning EAL include food items displaying text and labels in their home language.

Challenge some children to create a shopping list using sub-headings including dairy products, meat, fruit and so on.

Learning steps
- Use vocabulary focused on objects that are of particular importance to them, for example their favourite food.
- Use a widening range of words to express or elaborate on ideas.
- Extend vocabulary, especially by grouping and naming.
- Extend their vocabulary, exploring the meanings and sounds of new words.

Look, listen and note
How do they:
- use gestures and body language to convey meaning?
- recall and recount their own experiences and share them with other children?
- develop and extend their vocabulary, and what new words do they use?

ACTIVITY 22
Funny face biscuits

Vocabulary
feelings, happy, sad, angry, funny, scared

You will need
Round cracker biscuits, cheese spread, cut fruit and vegetables including raisins, cress, cucumber, carrots, grapes and so on (remember to find out about children's allergies), pencils and paper pads.

Online resources available

Ask the children to spread a cracker biscuit with cheese spread. Explain that they can then use the fruit and vegetable pieces to create different emotion faces on the cracker including happy, sad and so on.

Let them take turns to pretend to be customers, and waiters and waitresses taking orders using a pencil and pad. Extend their imaginative play and use of language by encouraging them to offer advice and options and to describe the different dishes.

Invite the children to eat their funny face biscuits.

Meeting different learners' needs

Support some children's understanding of the activity by using mirrors, persona dolls and symbols (see the 'Supporting children' section on pages 142–7) of different emotions to support their understanding of how they are feeling. Draw their attention to facial features of different emotions such as the shape of a mouth on a sad face and on their sad biscuit. Ensure that the children have the opportunity to talk about their emotions and feelings.

Provide children learning EAL with clear visual prompts such as photographs/symbols of faces displaying different emotions. Recognize non-verbal communication, such as gestures or actions, and praise and respond positively.

Challenge some children to elaborate on the emotions of the different biscuits, suggesting imaginary stories and explanations for why they are feeling that way.

Learning steps

- Are able to respond to simple requests and grasp meaning from context.
- Use language as a powerful means of widening contacts, and sharing feelings, experiences and thoughts.
- Begin to use talk to pretend in imaginary situations.
- Use talk to organize, sequence and clarify thinking, ideas, feelings and events.

Look, listen and note
How do they:

- use body language and some talk to support and think about what they are doing?
- use language in their pretend and imaginary play?
- (for children speaking languages other than English) use the language that is dominant, as well as gesture and intonation to convey meaning?

ACTIVITY 23
The Enormous Watermelon

Vocabulary
act, pull, watermelon, enormous, character

You will need
The book, *The Enormous Watermelon* by Brenda Parkes and Judith Smith (Mimosa), along with the following props: a green balloon (to represent the watermelon), a large seed, gardening tools, a bowl, spoon, long piece of rope, a box filled with brown paper made to look like a garden scene, watermelon pieces to taste, a dressing-up box.

Read the book, *The Enormous Watermelon*, over several sessions, with the children focusing on the language pattern and characters. Encourage the children to predict what will happen next while reading the story.

In a following activity, display a range of clothing from the dressing-up box. Invite the children to dress up as different characters. For example, a superhero, an animal, a queen, a fairy. Invite the children to suggest who their character is.

Retell the story with the new characters acting out their roles. Encourage the children to draw on the repetitive language used in the story, 'They pulled and pulled but they could not pull it home …'. Take photographs of the children dressed up acting out the story and use these in a later activity where they can create their own book.

Meeting different learners' needs

Support some children by showing them how to engage in role play through actions and using props to support their representational play. Repeat the activity over several sessions to provide children with the familiarity and confidence to use language in play. Encourage all the children to use various facial expressions in their play to support the understanding of children with hearing or communication difficulties.

For children learning EAL, provide opportunities to listen to the story recorded in their home language (either by a translator or a parent). Recognize non-verbal communication displayed through role play such as gestures, facial expression and actions. Praise and respond positively.

Challenge some children to add further changes to the story while maintaining the language pattern used in the original, for example by introducing a naughty character or by changing the ending of the story.

Learning steps
- Use action, sometimes with limited talk, that is largely concerned with the 'here and now'.
- Use talk to connect ideas, explain what is happening and anticipate what might happen next.
- Begin to use talk instead of action to rehearse, re-order and reflect on linking significant events from stories, paying attention to how events lead into one another.
- Use talk to organize, sequence and clarify thinking, ideas, feelings and events.

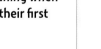

Look, listen and note
How do they:
- use actions and some talk to support and think about what they are doing?
- use talk to connect ideas and explain things?
- use language in their pretend and imaginary play?
- use gesture and intonation to convey meaning when English is not their first language?

ACTIVITY 24
Handa's Surprise!

Vocabulary
fruit, basket, walk, animals, character

You will need

The book, '*Handa's Surprise*' by Eileen Browne (Big Books) along with the following props: a basket, pampas or long grass, a picture/doll of Handa, real fruit/pictures of a mango, orange, banana, guava, pineapple, avocado, passion fruit and tangerine.

You will also need

Animal pictures/toys including a monkey, giraffe, zebra, gazelle, elephant, ostrich, giraffe, antelope and parrot.

Online resources available

Read the book, *Handa's Surprise!*, with the children. Talk about the title and explore the meaning of the word 'surprise'. What do the children think the surprise in the story might be?

Read the book using the objects to represent the story, and demonstrate reading skills such as tracking a finger from left to right and decoding words using phonics. Encourage the children to talk about what is happening in the story and to identify fruit that is unfamiliar to them. Also encourage the children to explore the multi-cultural aspects of the book. Some examples of discussion topics could be: its African setting; the various types of fruit in this story; and the different customs of this region. Use the pictures to identify the animals taking fruit without Handa knowing. Refer back to the title during the story, asking the children to predict what the surprise might be and how the story might end.

Once the story is finished, play a memory game using the fruit and basket. Ask the children to look at the basket full of fruit and try to remember what they can see. Cover the basket using the material and remove one of the pieces of fruit. Invite the children to identify which piece of fruit is missing.

Meeting different learners' needs

Support the children who may find memory tasks difficult by providing fewer pieces of fruit to begin with and by using pictures of the fruit as a visual prompt. Provide children with an opportunity and time to explore real items of fruit during the story and activity.

Support children learning EAL to access and interact with the story using story props, actions and gestures. Provide them with an opportunity to observe the game before asking them to take their turn as it may take some children a while to pick up the rules of the game.

Challenge some children to attempt to read unfamiliar words in the text using phonics as a prime approach to decode words.

Learning steps

- Listen to and join in with stories and poems, one to one and also in small groups.
- Suggest how a story might end.
- Show an interest in illustrations and print in books.
- Enjoy an increasing range of books.
- Show an understanding of the main elements of stories, such as main characters, sequences of events and openings.

Look, listen and note
How do they:

- respond to the story and explore the objects as you read with them?
- demonstrate an understanding of the elements of the story such as the setting, structure and ending?

All about me

There are so many literacy learning opportunities in this topic 'All about me'. From dressing up as our favourite superheroes to following instructions to dress a teddy, there's plenty of scope for active learning. Children develop respect and understanding of our differences and similarities by creating personalized poems, books about themselves, comparing how they've changed from a baby and by labelling a life-size body picture. We extend our vocabulary through games, describing activities, an imaginary visit to the doctor and making hilarious funny-face pictures.

Chapter contents

Role-play area ideas

These role-play areas will provide a fun and meaningful learning context for all learners:

- fancy-dress shop
- hat-and-wig stand
- doctor's surgery
- shoe shop
- clothes shop.

Songs and rhymes

- 'Head, shoulders, knees and toes, knees and toes'
- 'Put your finger on your ... on your ...'
- 'If you're happy and you know it ...'
- 'One finger one thumb keep moving ...'
- 'Teddy bear, teddy bear, touch your nose ...'

Hands-on learning

This chapter offers plenty of opportunities for hands-on learning, including dressing skills, joining in with action songs about the body, making face pictures and participating in role play. A visit from the local nurse or doctor can provide the children with a meaningful context on which to base their role play and active learning.

Parents as partners home activities

Ask parents and carers to send in their family photograph albums to share during circle time to develop children's confidence, communication and language skills. Also ask the children to bring in their favourite toy or teddy from home to display and share with the group.

Create 'All about me' passports and ask people at home to help to complete them. These can contain information about children's likes and dislikes, including their favourite food, colour and toys. It could also include a section about their family and friends. While all children will enjoy sharing their own passport, it is a particularly effective tool for supporting children with additional needs. For example, it may contain key Makaton signs a child uses or the specialist equipment they need. It can be used support both adults and children working with a child and is a great tool to support interaction and communication. Also useful are keywords from a child's home language or information about what comforts them if they become upset.

Links with the Early Learning Goals and EYFS

Personal, emotional and social development:

- Have a developing awareness of their own needs, views and feelings, and be sensitive to the needs, views and feelings of others.
- Understand that people have different needs, views, cultures and beliefs, which need to be treated with respect.
- Understand that they can expect others to treat their needs, views, cultures and beliefs with respect.

Knowledge and understanding of the world:

- Find out about, and identify, some features of living things, objects and events they observe.
- Find out about past and present events in their own lives, and in those of their families and other people they know.
- Find out about their environment, and talk about those features they like and dislike.

Physical development:

- Show awareness of space, of themselves and of others.

Creative development:

- Respond in a variety of ways to what they see, hear, smell, touch and feel.
- Express and communicate their ideas, thoughts and feelings by using a widening range of materials, suitable tools, imaginative role play, movement, designing and making and a variety of songs and musical instruments.

ACTIVITY 25
What am I doing?

You will need
Photographs of actions to be acted out such as hand washing, painting a picture, driving a car, riding a horse, pushing a wheelchair and so on.

Online resources available

Vocabulary
action, copy, same, different, guess, act, pretend

Invite the children to take it in turns to act out an activity such as jumping, clapping or hopping while everybody else must say what simple action each child is performing. Next, ask the children to work in pairs to act out an action photograph card using a series of different actions. For example, if the card shows a photograph of hand washing, the children could pretend to turn on the taps, wash their hands, turn the taps off and dry their hands on an imaginary towel. Invite the other children to ask questions and use talk to explain what they can see before guessing what they are doing.

Meeting different learners' needs

Support some children who may find it difficult to perform in front of other children by providing them with props and demonstrating appropriate actions for them to imitate.

Provide children learning EAL with time to observe the game before asking them to take their turn. Ensure that they have time to observe the photograph actions cards to support their understanding of the activity.

Challenge some children to talk about the sequence of events they observe, drawing on language such as 'first', 'last', 'next', 'before', 'after' and 'then'.

Learning steps
- Use simple statements and questions often linked to gestures.
- Respond to simple instructions.
- Use talk to gain attention and sometimes use actions rather than talk to explain to others.
- Interact with others, negotiating plans and activities and taking turns in conversation.
- Enjoy spoken and written language and turn it readily into their play and learning.

Look, listen and note
How do they:
- communicate in different ways?
- use language to talk about what they can see?

ACTIVITY 26
Look at me now

You will need
Photographs of the children
as babies and as they are
now, coloured paper (two pages per
child),squares of paper, glue sticks,
pens and Blu-tack.

Vocabulary
book, younger, older, remember, baby, changing

Display the photographs of the children as babies. Ask them to match the baby pictures with the recent photographs. Encourage the children to talk about their pictures. Can they remember being a baby? How have they changed?

Demonstrate how to make a simple flap page for the book by securing a photograph of the child as a baby onto a blank piece of paper using Blu-tack. Next carefully glue along one side of a flap and stick it in place to cover the baby photograph. Then secure the recent photograph on top of the flap.

Ask the children to draw a picture of themselves to add to the book and to attempt to write their name taking care to form the letters correctly. Organize the book so that each child has a double-page spread displaying his or her drawing and name on one side and the lift-up-flap page on the other. Give the book a title and share it with the children in following story-time sessions.

Meeting different learners' needs

Support some children who may have difficulties in drawing themselves to add their own marks/writing to their page even if this resembles scribble. Guide them to form or select clear large bold individual letters correctly to create their name.

This activity provides new children and children learning EAL with an opportunity to learn other children's names. Take care to pronounce children's names correctly.

Challenge some children to add their own writing in the form of a question to their page by writing a simple sentence such as 'Who is it?' Encourage them to form their letters correctly.

Learning steps
- Draw lines and circles using gross motor movements.
- Begin to use anticlockwise movement and retrace vertical lines.
- Begin to form recognizable letters.
- Use a pencil and hold it effectively to form recognizable letters, most of which are correctly formed.

Look, listen and note
How do they:
- control equipment and materials?
- form and write recognizable letters?

ACTIVITY 27
I like it!

Vocabulary
write, label, like, love, dislike, hate, best, favourite

You will need
A collection of children's things (toys, teddies, DVDs, clothing, food and so on), pens, crayons, scissors, magazines, catalogues, blank labels, feely bag, two hula-hoops, pictures or symbols (see the 'Supporting children' section on pages 142–7) of a happy and sad face.
Online resources available

Use a feely bag to create interest and anticipation by inviting the children to select an item from inside. Ask them to talk about what it is and whether they like or dislike it. Place the item into one of two hoops labelled with a happy face for 'like' or a sad face for 'dislike'. Encourage the children to recognize personal differences and how one person may place something in the 'like' hoop while someone else would not.

Support the children to write labels for the items explored, these can be added to a display. Encourage them to hold a pencil effectively to form recognizable letters correctly. Next ask the children to talk about and draw or write about their favourite thing.

Meeting different learners' needs

Support some children, who may have difficulties in drawing, to select pictures from magazines/catalogues of things that they like. Use images or objects that are personally significant to the children, such as a picture of mum or their family pet.

For children learning EAL provide them with happy and sad faces to support them in communicating their likes and dislikes.

Challenge some children to add a sentence about their favourite thing, for example 'I like chocolate'. Remind them to keep their letters a similar size.

Learning steps

- Use one-handed tools and equipment.
- Manipulate objects with increasing control.
- Begin to use anticlockwise movement and retrace vertical lines.
- Begin to form recognizable letters.
- Use a pencil and hold it effectively to form recognizable letters, most of which are correctly formed.

Look, listen and note

How do they:
- create different marks, lines and recognizable letters?
- hold and control a pencil or writing tool?
- form letters correctly?

ACTIVITY 28
A book about me

Vocabulary
hair, eyes, skin, height, celebrate, sentence, word, me

Ask the children to look in the mirror and compare differences in their appearance such as their hair and skin colour or whether they are tall or short. Encourage them to talk about and celebrate their differences. Ask the children to think about other differences that you cannot see in the mirror, for example different birthdays or religions.

You will need
Mirrors, glue sticks, blank pages/books, a selection of scrap material of varying textures and colours, scissors, crayons, coloured pencils, pictures/photographs of various celebrations such as festivals, birthdays and family occasions (you can ask parents and carers to bring in photographs from home prior to this session).

You will also need
Pictures/photographs/packaging of different types of food that the children like to eat.

Online resources available

Show the children examples of different books that look at differences in our appearance. Explain that they are going to make a book all about themselves. Write one sentence for each page, for examples 'The colour of my hair is ...' (the children glue a piece of coloured paper to match their hair here); 'The colour of my eyes is ...'; 'I like to eat ...'; 'I like to celebrate ...'. Each child should contribute by completing the sentence with suitable textures, colours, pictures or simple words.

Meeting different learners' needs

Support some children who are not able to write letters or words by providing them with an opportunity to observe you scribing their ideas. Focus on them selecting textures, colours and packaging to record their ideas rather than words.

For children learning EAL, use examples of food packaging displaying print from their home language to develop their understanding of different forms of writing to record their ideas.

Challenge some children to form simple words and sentences to record their ideas.

ACTIVITY 29
Words about me

You will need

Dressing-up box, adjective word cards to describe the characteristics of different people/characters, for example rich, caring, scary, beautiful, brave, dangerous or helpful.

Online resources available

Vocabulary

describe, person, pretend, act, dress up, guess

Display a selection of clothes in front of the children. Explain that they are going to be dressing up as different characters. Invite each child to select a describing card and think about what sort of clothes that person might wear, for example a child could dress up as a nurse for a card displaying 'caring'.

Invite the children to dress up as a character using the description on their card. Once the children are dressed invite each child to come to the front of the class and act out their character. The rest of the children guess who they think they are impersonating. Use the activity to encourage a discussion about using different words to describe themselves.

Meeting different learners' needs

Support some children to help them to read the word on the card. Provide them with simple choices to support their understanding of the activity, for example 'Would a rich person wear jewels or rags?'

It may take time for children learning EAL to understand and recognize representational play. Provide them with the opportunity to play and explore objects and props while asking them what the objects could be used for.

Challenge some children to extend their use of language to take on the roles of different characters, for example asking them to think about what language a caring person would use?

Learning steps
- Use actions and a small amount of talk that is largely concerned with the 'here and now'.
- Talk activities through, reflecting on and modifying what they are doing.
- Begin to use talk in imaginary situations.
- Use language to imagine and recreate roles and experiences.

Look, listen and note
How do they:
- use actions and some talk to support what they are doing?
- show that they understand, by what they do and say?

ACTIVITY 30
Dress the teddy

You will need
Teddies, different coloured outfits to dress the teddies in, such as hats, vests, tops, trousers, skirts, shorts, dresses, socks, shoes and so on (old baby clothes make good outfits), a spinner/die displaying colours which correspond to the coloured clothing for the teddies.

Vocabulary
colour, change, dress, match, first, last, next, before, after

Explain that the children will be playing a game to see who can dress their teddy first. Ask the children to work in pairs. Each pair takes a turn to select a colour using the spinner or die. They must then find an item of clothing which is the same colour and dress the bear in that item. If there is no clothing of a particular colour left, the children must miss a turn. Additionally, the children must carefully plan the order in which they dress the bear. For example, they must add the teddy's socks before they put on his shoes. Encourage them to develop their use of language to negotiate and sequence events during the activity, for example 'We need his vest first'. The winning pair is the first to dress their teddy from head to toe.

Meeting different learners' needs

Support some children who may struggle with their fine manipulation by pairing them with another child who will help them as opposed to taking over during the activity. A switch accessible spinner can be used by all children during the game, including those with gross or fine motor difficulties (see the 'Supporting children' section on pages 142–7 for further details).

When introducing the activity use mime and gesture to support language development for children learning EAL. The practical context of the activity will help them to learn new words.

Challenge some children to speak clearly and audibly with control and confidence, and show an awareness of the listener.

Learning steps

- Use simple statements often linked to gestures.
- Listen to others in one-to-one situations or small groups when the conversation interests them.
- Respond to simple instructions.
- Begin to use more complex sentences.
- Interact with others, negotiating plans and activities and turn taking in conversation.
- Enjoy listening to and using spoken language and turn it readily into their play and learning.

Look, listen and note
How do they:

- use actions and some talk to support what they are doing?
- demonstrate an awareness of conventions such as taking turns to talk?

ACTIVITY 31
Funny faces

Vocabulary
sound, match, same, listen, letter, word

You will need
A blank face template for each child cut out of card/paper, pictures of facial features taken from magazines/photocopies to add to their template, glue sticks, textured material to add to their picture to create jewellery, beards, hair and moustaches.

Online resources available

Explain that the children will be thinking about the sound at the beginning of a word. Play a game of 'I spy' with the children to encourage them to recognize and use the initial letter sound of different facial features such as 'I spy with my little eye something beginning with nnn – nose.'

Prompt the children to find a feature to stick onto their face picture by giving the initial sound, for example 'Funny face needs an "m".' The children find something beginning with that sound, such as 'mouth', and stick it onto their picture. Repeat using different letters and sounds until their funny face is complete.

Meeting different learners' needs

Support some children by providing them with mirrors to aid their understanding. Focus on helping them to follow simple instructions and to name or point to different facial features.

Children learning EAL generally hear sounds in spoken words very easily, however it may be useful to learn some keywords such as 'listen' and 'look' in a child's home language and use these to support their understanding during the activity.

Challenge some children to use their phonic knowledge to suggest more complicated sound blends and words such as 'ear'.

Learning steps
- Distinguish one sound from another.
- Show interest in play with sounds.
- Hear and say the initial sound in words and know which letters represent some of the sounds.
- Link sounds to letters, naming and sounding the letters of the alphabet.

Look, listen and note
How do they:
- use and understand language during the activity?
- demonstrate knowledge of the initial sounds at the beginning of words?
- use their phonic knowledge?

ACTIVITY 32
Label me!

You will need
A long roll or piece of paper,
crayons/pencils and labels.
Online resources available

> **Vocabulary**
> body, label, word, name, various body parts

Begin the session by singing some familiar songs about the body such as 'Head, shoulders, knees and toes' and 'You put your left leg in, your left leg out'.

Invite one of the children to lie down on top of the paper with his or her legs together and arms slightly spread. Ask the other children to draw around his or her outline.

Display the outline and help the children to write labels to add to the drawing to identify the different parts of the body, such as the head, leg, arm and so on. The children can then work together to add collage materials and features to the outline to bring the drawing to life, for example by adding long pieces of black wool for the hair and squares of pink material in the shape of a skirt.

Meeting different learners' needs

Support some children who may struggle to write a word by asking them to select a picture or a symbol (see the 'Supporting children' section on pages 142–7) or to draw a specific part of the body to use as a label.

Children learning EAL can also use pictures or symbols as labels. Welcome their contributions in their primary language, including attempts at writing in different scripts, as they are still developing their understanding of using text to label a drawing/picture.

Challenge some children to attempt more complex words using their phonic knowledge, for example 'elbow', 'thumb', 'knee' and so on.

Learning steps

- Distinguish between the different marks they make.
- Sometimes give meaning to marks as they draw and paint.
- Use their phonic knowledge to write simple regular words and make phonetically plausible attempts at more complex words.
- Write labels and captions.

Look, listen and note
How do they:
- talk about what they have written/drawn?
- use writing to create a label?
- make use of phonic knowledge to attempt to write words?

ACTIVITY 33
I am special

Vocabulary
poem, describe, body, face, word, colour, me, like, I

Read the poem 'I am special' (below) to the children. Model to them how to trace your finger from left to right, top to bottom following the text as you read. Encourage them to talk about their own differences and similarities, for example differences in skin, eye or hair colour.

I am special

Here is my picture for everyone to see,
Nobody else looks exactly like me,
My eyes are brown they're different you see,
My laughter, my smile are special to me.
My skin, my hair, my nose and feet
Make my features quite unique.
Here is my picture for everyone to see,
It's really quite nice being special like me.

Ask them to draw a picture of themselves. Help them to read a range of words and phrases and to add them to their picture to describe themselves.

Meeting different learners' needs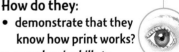

Support some children who may find it difficult to draw a picture by using a photograph of themselves and supporting them to read words to add to their photograph. Also use a mirror to support them in recognizing their own features and reflection.

For children learning EAL, ask a qualified bilingual adult or parent to translate the poem and record it onto a switch/audio recorder. Use the poem to support parent link activities and encourage them to listen to the poem several times during the activity.

Challenge some children to read sections of the poem without support.

Learning steps
- Listen to and join in with poems, one to one and also in small groups.
- Know that information can be relayed in the form of print.
- Understand the concept of a word.
- Explore and experiment with sounds, words and texts.
- Know that print carries meaning and, in English, is read from left to right, top to bottom.

Look, listen and note
How do they:
- demonstrate that they know how print works?
- use phonic skills to decide text?
- recognize or read some words?

ACTIVITY 34
Make a letter

You will need
A camera, PE mats, letter flash cards and foam/plastic letters.

Online resources available

Vocabulary
letter, sound, straight, curved, round, stretch, bend, long

Display the letters for the children to see and play a game of 'I spy' to develop their awareness of the different sounds linked to each letter. Talk about how the different letters are formed and encourage the children to 'feel' the shape of the letter sounds by tracing their fingers over different letters.

Ask the children in small groups to take turns to see what different letters they can make with their bodies. Encourage them to work together to create some letters, such as one long straight child's body joined onto another child who is curled up into a ball for 'p'.

Take photographs of the children's different letter shapes. Encourage them to look at, talk about and draw each other's ideas. In a following session, display the photographs and encourage the children to match different foam/plastic letters while thinking about the different sounds for each letter.

Meeting different learners' needs

Ensure all the children have the opportunity to join in with this activity. Provide a clear area on a PE mat for children with physical difficulties to move freely and safely. Support children who are not yet familiar with letters to recognize when letter shapes or sounds are different and when they match.

Provide children learning EAL with time to observe and understand the activity before asking them to take their turn.

Challenge some children to spell simple regular words using a combination of photographs of letter shapes.

Learning steps
- Distinguish one sound from another.
- Link sounds to letters, naming and sounding the letters of the alphabet.

Look, listen and note
How do they:
- use and understand their primary language?
- recognize different letter sounds and shapes?
- link sounds to letters?

ACTIVITY 35
Doctor! Doctor!

Vocabulary
medicine, injection, bandage, ill, healthy

You will need
A doctor's role-play area, including doctors' instruments such as stethoscope, bandages, play thermometer, syringe, medicine and so on.

You will also need
Leaflets, posters and notices, waiting room area, dolls, teddies, magazines for the waiting room, reception desk and equipment.

Introduce the doctor's role-play area to the children by modelling to them appropriate language, gestures and actions. For example, 'Good morning, what seems to be the problem?' Ask the children, What do doctors do? How do they make us better? Who has been to the doctor?

Encourage the children to take on different roles and act out imaginary scenarios in character using the dolls and teddies. Encourage them to talk about what is happening.

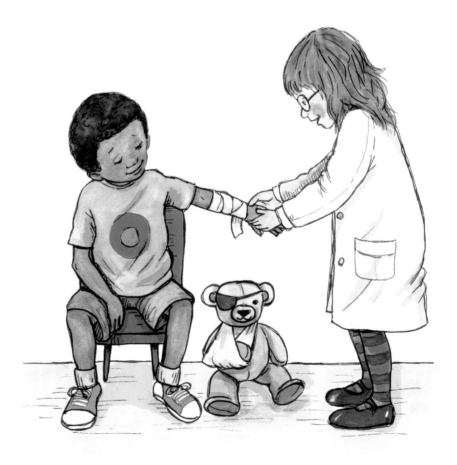

Meeting different learners' needs

Support some children by providing them with a running commentary to describe what you are doing, using gestures, actions and props to give added meaning. Provide them with props to support their role-play skills. Encourage the children to use all of their senses during the activity, such as listening for a heart beat, touching and exploring different role-play resources and smelling different safe medical creams such as Sudacrem. Voice output devices and symbols (see the 'Supporting children' section on pages 142-7) can be used to support the existing communication of children with speech and language or hearing difficulties.

Encourage children speaking languages other than English to use gestures and actions to support their communication skills. Value and welcome their contributions in their home language as well as attempts at new words and vocabulary.

Challenge some children to work in pairs using talk to cooperate, organize and clarify their ideas.

Learning steps
- Use action, sometimes with limited talk, that is largely connected with the here and now.
- Use language as a means of widening contacts, and sharing feelings, experiences and thoughts.
- Talk activities through, reflecting on and modifying what the children are doing.
- Use language to imagine and recreate roles and experiences.
- Use talk to organize sequence and clarify ideas, feelings and events.

Look, listen and note
How do they:
- show that they understand?
- use language (including signs, symbols and gestures) in pretend and imaginary play?
- (for children speaking languages others than English) develop and use their dominant language, as well as gesture and intonation to convey meaning?

ACTIVITY 36
My family

Vocabulary
family, house, home, pet, dog, cat, mum, dad, me, name, read

You will need

A sheet titled 'My family' for each child, lower-case word labels for each family member including, dad, mum, pet, cat, dog, granddad, sister, brother, cousin, uncle and so on (remember that the children may use different names for people in their family such as nana or grandma), word labels displaying each child's name and glue sticks.

Online resources available

Ask the children to talk about who is in their family and who lives in their house. Explain that they are going to draw their immediate family members and add word labels.

Support them to read the words on the labels using their phonic knowledge and recognition of some common words. Remind the children not to forget to add themselves, and to find their name and add it to their picture.

Meeting different learners' needs

Support some children by using photographs of their family members and asking them to add these to their picture to support their understanding and to make this activity more meaningful. Support them to match and read short simple words such as 'mum' and 'dad'.

Children learning EAL may have other family members overseas who they might wish to talk about or include in their picture. Welcome their contributions and use photographs where appropriate.

Challenge some children to read unfamiliar, more challenging words such as 'grandma' and 'auntie'. Some children can also use this as an opportunity to develop their understanding of using capital letters for names/titles by changing the first letter in the title to a capital for example, 'grandma' becomes 'Grandma'.

Learning steps
- Understand the concept of a word.
- Explore and experiment with sounds, words and texts.
- Read a range of familiar and common words independently.

Look, listen and note
How do they:
- demonstrate that they know how print works?
- use phonic skills to decode text?
- recognize or read some words?

Opposites

This chapter offers lots of hands-on experience to link various opposite concepts with meaningful and fun literacy activities. Listening skills are developed while making shakers, playing listening games, investigating what's inside the box and listening for animals that lurk in the night. Understanding of everyday opposites in our environment is developed through outdoor learning, imaginative play at the seaside and post office and by helping to tidy up mess in the garden centre.

Chapter contents

Role-play area ideas

Various opposite concepts can be explored in a meaningful context through the following role-play areas:

- post office (big/small, heavy/light, in/out)
- shoe shop (long/short, big/small, on/off, in/out)
- garden centre (full/empty, dirty/clean, up/down)
- dark cave (light/dark, in/out, night/day)
- seaside (wet/dry, land/sea, float/sink).

Songs and rhymes

Further songs can be created by altering the words to familiar tunes:

- 'The Grand Old Duke of York' (up and down)
- 'Hickory Dickory Dock' (up and down)
- 'I hear thunder' (loud and quiet).

Hands-on learning

Through outdoor learning opportunities, explore opposite concepts in meaningful contexts, for example visit a real garden centre or post office, and find opposites in the home, playground and around the centre or school during opposite hunts and adventures.

Ensure as much hands-on learning as possible with this topic by using the adult-led literacy activities suggested in this chapter as a starting point for free-play and child-directed learning. Provide plenty of opportunities for exploration of the water tray, sand-play, shakers and instruments as well as the garden and post office role-play areas, and use this opportunity to observe how the children engage with the activities.

Parents as partners home activities

Ask the children with parents and carers at home to explore their house to see what opposites they can find. Change the theme each week, for example when thinking about the opposites 'young' and 'old' they could bring in a picture of one of their grandparents as a young baby and a more recent picture as an older adult. For the opposites float and sink they could bring in something from home that they found to sink and something that floated. Encourage the children to share and talk about what they did and add their objects to a display.

Invite the children to an 'opposites day' where they must come to school dressed in opposites, for example one white sock and one black or half of their hair up and the other down.

Links with the Early Learning Goals and EYFS

Problem solving, reasoning and numeracy:

- Use language such as 'greater', 'smaller', 'heavier' or 'lighter' to compare quantities.
- Use everyday words to describe position.

Knowledge and understanding of the world:

- Find out about, and identify, some features of living things, objects and events they observe.
- Look closely at similarities, differences, patterns and change.
- Investigate objects and materials by using all of their senses as appropriate.

Creative development:

- Express and communicate their ideas, thoughts and feelings by using a widening range of materials, suitable tools, imaginative role play, movement, designing and making and a variety of songs and musical instruments.
- Recognize and explore how sounds can be changed, sing simple songs from memory, recognize repeated sounds and sound patterns and match movements to music.
- Use their imagination in art and design, music, dance, role play and stories.

ACTIVITY 37
Jack's opposite playing cards

Vocabulary
giant, small, rich, poor, happy, sad, angry, excited, old, young

You will need

The book, *Jack and the Beanstalk*, along with the following props: cards displaying the words used to describe different opposites that occur throughout the story (see vocabulary for examples), magic beans (broad beans painted and covered in glitter), a toy cow, gold coins, a toy axe, a long vine (tissue paper twisted around pipe cleaners with felt leaves), a texture picture of a castle in the clouds (with cotton-wool clouds) and a model run-down house/texture picture.

Online resources available

Read the book, *Jack and the Beanstalk*, several times with the children. Discuss the main features of the story and model how to read the book tracing your finger from left to right, top to bottom. Ask the children to think about different opposites that occur throughout the story, for example a big giant and a small boy. Support them to use their phonic knowledge to decode and read word cards that describe the opposites, for example 'this word begins with "s", s – a – d'.

Next ask each child to draw two opposite scenarios from the story, one on each side of a large playing card. With support, help them to read and select a word to add to each picture to describe it. For example, adding the word 'sad' to a picture of a cow on its way to be sold, while, on the other side of the card, adding the word 'happy' to a picture of Jack and his mother with all their riches at the end of the story.

The children can use their playing cards in follow-on activities such as guess the mime and snap.

Meeting different learners' needs

Support some children to distinguish text from illustrations and encourage them to point to features in a picture. For children who are not able to draw for themselves, provide pictures of the characters to colour in. You can also use enhanced facial expressions and props such as emotions puppets or dressing-up clothes to give added meaning when telling the story and drawing the children's attention to different opposites within the story.

Provide children with EAL with clear visual cues to support their understanding. Also use dual-language books or invite parents/carers or qualified bilingual adults to read the story in the language used at home.

Challenge some children to read short sentences.

Learning steps

- Know information can be relayed in the form of print.
- Understand the concept of a word.
- Explore and experiment with sounds, words and texts.
- Read a range of familiar and common words and simple sentences independently.
- Know that print carries meaning and, in English, is read from left to right and top to bottom.

Look, listen and note

How do they:

- attempt to read different words?
- make reference to and understand how print works, for example do they begin tracing the word/sentence from the left?

ACTIVITY 38

Shake it!

Vocabulary
loud, quiet, shaker, listen, silent, noisy

You will need
Various empty containers with lids, two large boxes – one with a picture to represent 'quiet' (such as someone saying 'shhh') and one for 'loud' (such as someone covering their ears), a variety of 'quiet' and 'loud' materials to fill them with, for example cotton wool, string, pieces of fabric, paper, pebbles, pasta, rice and so on.
Online resources available

Introduce the activity by inviting the children to choose a container. Demonstrate that the empty containers make no noise when shaken. Explain that by filling them with different materials they can make their own 'shakers'.

Invite the children to explore the different materials and discuss whether they think it would make a loud or quiet noise inside a shaker, for example 'Would cotton wool make a loud or quiet noise?'

Ask the children to work in pairs. Give each pair one specific material to fill their shaker with, such as pebbles or pieces of fabric. Encourage the children to explore each other's shakers and sort them into the 'loud' and 'quiet' boxes.

Once the children have sorted the shakers take one from the box and play it rhythmically using gestures while altering the volume of your voice, for example whispering, 'Quiet – quiet – quiet ... quiet – quiet – quiet' while encouraging the children to whisper along or shouting 'Loud – loud – loud'.

Meeting different learners' needs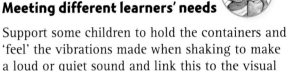

Support some children to hold the containers and 'feel' the vibrations made when shaking to make a loud or quiet sound and link this to the visual cues for loud and quiet.

Children learning EAL will have clear visual cues to support their understanding in this activity. Use gestures such as a finger to lips for 'quiet' and hands over ears for 'loud'.

Challenge some children to hear and say the sounds in words used to describe loud and quiet in the order in which they occur for example 'l – ou – d'.

Learning steps
- Distinguish one sound from another.
- Show an interest in play with sounds and rhythms.
- Hear and say the sounds in words.

Look, listen and note
How do they:
- discriminate and reproduce sounds?
- listen and respond during the activity?

ACTIVITY 39
Night and day

Vocabulary
animal, insect, night, day, dark, light, asleep, awake

You will need
The book, *Animals Day and Night* by Katharine Kenah (School Specialty Publishing), along with the following props: a large piece of black material, pictures or models of animals/insects from the book.

Online resources available

Create a dark den using the material and invite the children to sit inside for the activity. Read the book, *Animals Day and Night*, with a small group of children. Encourage them to help to name the animals and think of what sounds they would make. Explain that this type of book is used to find out information rather than tell a story.

Ask the children to select animals and insects to add to the night-time den. Encourage them to refer to the pages of the book to find out the information they need by prompting them with questions, for example 'Should the bat go in the night-time den?'

Meeting different learners' needs

Support some children by using animal actions and sound effects where appropriate, providing them with time to explore model animals and the pictures in the book.

Children learning EAL may be unfamiliar with British native animals or may use different sounds and words to describe them. Record real animal sound effects for the children to listen to while in the night-time den. Welcome their contributions.

Challenge some children to sound out and attempt to read words in the book using their knowledge of phonics and letters.

Learning steps

- Show interest in illustrations and print in books and print in the environment.
- Know information can be relayed in the form of print.
- Enjoy an increasing range of books.
- Know that information can be retrieved from books and computers.
- Know that print carries meaning and, in English, is read from left to right and top to bottom.
- Show an understanding of the elements of stories, such as the main character, sequence of events and openings, and how information can be found in non-fiction texts to answer questions about where, who, why and how.

Look, listen and note

How do they:

- demonstrate an understanding of using books to find information?
- use non-fiction books?
- use a book to answer questions?

ACTIVITY 40
Outdoor opposites

Vocabulary
fast, slow, stop, go, forwards, backwards

You will need

Access to a safe age-appropriate playground and play equipment such as a see-saw, a roundabout, swings and a slide.

While visiting a park, encourage the children to identify opposites linked to movement and the equipment they use. For example, using the terms 'stop' and 'go' when on the roundabout or 'fast' and 'slow' when on the swings. Encourage the children to talk about their experiences and further develop their vocabulary by using sound effects linked to movement such as 'zoom!' and 'whoosh!'

Meeting different learners' needs

Support some children's understanding and expression of their experiences by using gestures, signing and picture symbols. Ensure that all have an opportunity to access the play equipment and resources (specialized disability equipment can be found in a range of centres and special schools).

For children learning EAL this first-hand experience will provide an excellent stimulus for language development. Use simple instructions such as 'stop' and 'go' accompanied by hand gestures to emphasize meaning. Remember to recognize non-verbal communication with praise and respond to it positively.

Challenge some children to extend their vocabulary by using new words linked to an activity such as 'speedy' or 'swift' to describe fast movement and 'sluggish' or 'steady' to describe slow movement.

Learning steps

- Use language linked to first-hand experiences.
- Use words linked to an experience during play.
- Extend their vocabulary exploring the meaning and sounds of new words.

Look, listen and note
How do they:

- use their first language (including foreign languages, signing or other) with their peers and adults?
- interact with others (these may be culturally or behaviourally determined)?
- use gestures and body language to communicate?
- use a variety and range of words in play?

ACTIVITY 41
At the post office

Vocabulary
letter, parcel, post box, stamp, stick, big, small, heavy, light, send, collect

You will need
A post-office role-play area, including letters and parcels of various sizes and weight, post box, stamps and ink pad, play car/van, sacks, stamps and stickers, scales, cash register and money.

Explain that the children will be at the post office and have lots of jobs to do. Ask them to suggest ideas for what needs to be done by the postmen and postladies. Support them to think about different opposites at the post office. For example, 'We need to sort the letters into small and big ones.' Encourage the children to take on different roles and engage in imaginative play.

Meeting different learners' needs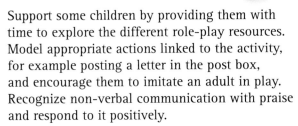

Support some children by providing them with time to explore the different role-play resources. Model appropriate actions linked to the activity, for example posting a letter in the post box, and encourage them to imitate an adult in play. Recognize non-verbal communication with praise and respond to it positively.

It may take time for children learning EAL to understand and recognize representational play. Provide the children with the opportunity to play and explore objects, props and the role-play corner, and talk about and show what the objects could be used for while emphasizing keywords.

Challenge some children to extend their communication by taking on different characters and using different voice styles during role play. For example, acting as an unhappy customer complaining about a missing letter.

Learning steps
- Are able to respond to simple requests and grasp meaning from context.
- Use talk to connect ideas, explain what is happening and anticipate what might happen next.
- Begin to use talk to pretend imaginary situations.
- Use language to imagine and recreate roles and experiences.

Look, listen and note
How do they:
- show that they understand the activity by what they do and say, for example the actions, questions and words they use?
- use language in their pretend play?
- for children using alternative languages such as sign/symbol communication or those speaking languages other than English, note which language is dominant, as well as their use of gesture and intonation to convey meaning.

ACTIVITY 42
What's in the box?

You will need

Opaque soap boxes, sticky tape and a variety of everyday objects and materials, for example coins, rice, cotton wool, ice cubes, play dough, water, sand, pebbles and so on.

Online resources available

> **Vocabulary**
> shake, listen, describe, talk, guess, hear

Hide different objects and materials in opaque soap boxes and seal them with tape. Invite the children to shake and listen to the objects inside. Use questions about opposites to encourage the children to describe and work out what they think is inside the box, for example 'Is it hard or soft, solid or liquid, heavy or light?' Their response might be, 'It sounds hard, it might be a penny.' Encourage them to work together and share their ideas.

During the plenary of this session the boxes can be opened and the children can help to evaluate whether they guessed correctly.

Meeting different learners' needs

Support some children to use all of their senses to enhance their learning opportunities. Provide photographs/pictures/symbols (see the 'Supporting children' on pages 142–7) of the items inside to provide them with a visual prompt and aid the communication during the activity. Also semi-translucent boxes can be used for hearing impaired children and can be used to make the guessing game easier.

For children learning EAL use simple language and emphasize the keywords used in this activity. For less confident children ensure that they have had ample opportunity to observe others playing the game before asking them to take their turn.

Challenge some children to negotiate their ideas and take turns independently when working with others. Provide them with boxes that are more challenging to describe and categorize. For example, an ice cube that will begin to melt during the activity.

Learning steps

- Learn new words and are able to use them in communicating about matters that interest them.
- Listen to others in one-to-one situations or small groups when conversation interests them.
- Use a widening range of words to express or elaborate on ideas.
- Extend vocabulary, especially by grouping and naming.
- Interact with others, negotiating plans and activities and taking turns in conversation.

Look, listen and note
How do they:

- begin to use new words?
- use a variety of words to describe opposites and objects?
- take turns in conversation and show an awareness of the listener?

ACTIVITY 43
My book of opposites

Vocabulary
hard, soft, rough, smooth, shiny, dull

Show the children examples of books about opposites and let them explore and identify some opposites for themselves. Using a feely bag, invite different children to take an item and describe it. Ask the children to describe what they have found using open-ended questions such as 'How does it feel?' Once the children have taken all of the objects from the bag encourage them to find pairs of opposite objects such as a soft toy and a hard piece of Lego or a light feather and a heavy stone. Children may classify the same objects using different words and opposites such as a soft feather and a hard stone. Welcome all contributions and use this as a platform for discussion.

Ask the children, while working in small groups, to choose two opposite objects and stick them onto a piece of card. Ask them to describe each object and help them to form a simple sentence and write it, for example 'The pebble is hard', 'The sponge is soft'.

Meeting different learners' needs

Support some children by scribing a sentence for them and asking them to add their own 'writing' which may be random marks that they ascribe meaning to.

Use simple language for children learning EAL and remember that many descriptive words used to describe opposites may be new to them and not part of the everyday English they usually hear.

Challenge some children to add punctuation to their sentence such as capital letters and full stops.

Learning steps
- Examine the writing that others make.
- Sometimes give meaning to marks as they draw and paint.
- Begin to break the flow of speech into words.
- Use writing as a means of recording and communicating.
- Write their own names and other things such as labels and captions, and begin to form simple sentences, sometimes using punctuation.

Look, listen and note
How do they:
- demonstrate an interest in the marks they make?
- break the flow of speech into a simple sentence?
- write words or sentences?

ACTIVITY 44
Opposites out at sea

You will need
Water tray, sand and water play toys such as boats, sea creatures, fish and play people.

Vocabulary
wet, dry, land, sea, rough, calm

Invite the children to create a seaside landscape using a water tray, sand and other resources. Model the use of language to talk ideas through and modify what they are doing. Encourage them to recognize opposites linked to seaside imaginative play, for example 'Put the man in the boat ... oh no ... the boat is too small ... I'll get a bigger boat.'

Encourage them to use their imagination and develop communication skills by using objects to represent other things. For example, a simple lollypop stick can become a lighthouse to warn sailors of dangerous rocks during rough seas.

Meeting different learners' needs

Support some children by helping them to explore the water tray and resources. Use simple language largely connected to the here and now, for example 'Can you find the boat?' Also use gestures and actions to support communication and language skills.

For children learning EAL recognize non-verbal communication, praise it and respond to it positively. Children must not be discouraged from using their home language as it will support their overall development and learning.

Challenge some children to use talk to tell an imaginative story using the water tray and resources.

Learning steps

- Use action, sometimes with limited talk, that is largely concerned to the here and now.
- Talk activities through, reflecting on and modifying what they are doing.
- Use talk to give new meanings to objects and actions, treating them as symbols for other things.
- Use talk to organize, sequence and clarify thinking, ideas, feelings and events.

Look, listen and note
How do they:

- use talk or communicate with others to support what they are doing?
- (for children using alternative languages such as sign/symbol communication or those speaking languages other than English) use gesture and intonation to convey meaning, and which language is dominant?
- use language in their pretend and imaginary play?

ACTIVITY 45
Stop and go

Vocabulary
stop, go, listen, play, instrument, loud, quiet, fast, slow

You will need

Musical instruments, a traffic controller hat, Blu-tack, a traffic sign (this can be made from two paper plates attached to a cardboard roll and painted in contrasting colours), pairs of picture cards which can be Blu-tacked onto the traffic sign to represent opposites, for example a picture of a hare with the word 'fast' underneath and a picture of a tortoise with the word 'slow' underneath; other cards may include 'loud', 'quiet', 'stop', 'go' and so on.

Online resources available

Ask a small group of children to sit in a circle facing you. Explain that they are going to play a game where they must play their instrument by following the instruction displayed on the traffic sign, for example when you display the 'fast' picture and word card the children must play their instruments fast.

Repeat the game using different pairs of opposites, encouraging the children to distinguish between the sounds they make.

Let's All Play

Meeting different learners' needs

Support some children by helping them to explore the different instruments and make some sounds independently. Focus on one pair of opposites such as 'stop' and 'go' to support their understanding through repetition.

Provide children learning EAL with clear visual cues to support their understanding in this activity. Use gestures such as holding up a flat hand for 'stop' and pointing for 'go'. Multi-cultural instruments familiar to the child can also be used where available.

Challenge some children by sticking different letters onto the traffic sign and asking the children to sound out the letters and sound blends.

Learning steps

- To distinguish one sound from another.
- To show an interest in play with sounds.
- Enjoy rhythmic activities.
- Link sounds to letters, naming and sounding the letters of the alphabet.

Look, listen and note
How do they:

- identify, make and talk about the opposite sounds?
- listen and respond as the instrument is being played?

ACTIVITY 46
Tidy up that mess!

You will need

Various pieces of card folded to create blank labels, a selection of pens, pencils and crayons, a garden-centre role-play area including garden items such as plants, flowers, pots, hanging baskets, rakes, trowels, soil, seeds, watering cans, gloves, aprons, hose pipe, posters, pictures and so on.

Online resources available

Vocabulary
label, word, write, tidy, messy, organize, sort

Introduce the activity in a garden-centre role-play area. Display a jumbled collection of items. Explain that the children will be helping out in the garden centre by thinking about the opposites 'tidy' and 'messy'. They will be clearing up the jumble of items and writing labels to organize and tidy it.

Model how to write a label using phonics to sound out and write different words for example, 'p – o – t – s'. Invite the children to work together to organize and tidy the area. Support them to create labels by drawing a picture of a garden item (easier) or by writing a word using their phonic knowledge (harder).

This activity can be revisited over several sessions to encourage the children to tidy up after themselves by reading the labels they have made.

Meeting different learners' needs

Support some children by using real objects such as real plants as opposed to artificial ones. For those who are not able to write words or draw pictures on their labels, ask them to select a pre-cut picture/photograph/symbol (see the 'Supporting children' section on pages 142–7) and stick it onto a label card.

Use simple language for children learning EAL and display examples of labels in different languages, some of which may be more familiar to them, to develop their understanding of the purpose of a label, for example on food packaging.

Challenge some children to create other examples of writing for the role-play area such as posters, instructions or signs.

Learning steps

- Sometimes give meaning to marks as they draw and paint.
- Use writing as a means of recording and communicating.
- Attempt writing for different purposes, using features of different forms such as lists, stories and instructions.
- Write labels and captions.

Look, listen and note
How do they:
- ascribe meaning to the mark they make?
- demonstrate an understanding of the purpose of labels?

ACTIVITY 47
Roll it!

You will need

A range of balls including bean-bag balls, hard balls, soft balls, big and small balls, long pieces of paper, outside area/large tray, paints, trays, an old pipe cut in half.

Vocabulary

roll, line, long, short, curved, straight, ball

Begin the session by asking each child to choose a ball. Ask them to explore and describe it by prompting them with questions related to opposites such as 'Is it a big or small ball?' Encourage the children to develop their manipulation skills, for example throwing, catching and rolling the balls.

Demonstrate how to dip a ball into the paint and roll it along the paper. Talk about the marks that are made, for example are they straight or curved, long or short? Invite the children to explore mark-making using different balls and coloured paints.

Meeting different learners' needs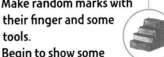

Support some children by engaging them in activities which develop their hand–eye coordination such as catching a ball that is rolled to them, or turning and exploring various balls using both their hands. For children who are unable to hold or roll a ball, use a soft ball that is easier to grip, with a 'shoot' to enable the ball to roll down and along the paper (this can be made from an old pipe cut in half).

Provide children learning EAL with clear visual cues and use simple language to support their understanding.

Challenge some children to form some letters correctly by rolling the ball in different directions.

Learning steps

- Make random marks with their finger and some tools.
- Begin to show some control in their use of tools and equipment.
- Manipulate objects with increasing control.
- Begin to form recognizable letters.

Look, listen and note
How do they:

- develop their fine motor skills?
- control equipment and talk about the marks they have made?

ACTIVITY 48
Letter lucky dip

Vocabulary
letter, sound, same, different, trace, copy, write

You will need
A large sand pit/tray, small shallow trays (such as old baking trays), sieves, buckets, two sets of foam or plastic letters, sand play tools and equipment such as sieves, rakes, buckets, trowels and so on.

Explain that the children will be thinking about the opposites 'same' and 'different' by finding pairs of letters hidden in the sand and practising writing them. Invite the children to explore the large sand tray to find and match the letters using the sand play tools and equipment.

Invite the children to copy the different letters in the small sand trays using their finger. Support them to form letters correctly using anticlockwise movements and retracing vertical lines.

Meeting different learners' needs

Support some children by asking them to make random marks in the sand using their hands and other tools. Develop their hand–eye coordination when looking for hidden letters and use visual cues such as finger spelling, large bold flash cards or feel the texture and shape of plastic or foam letters to support their understanding.

Provide children learning EAL with clear visual cues and use simple language to support their understanding.

Challenge some children to write words in the sand.

Learning steps

- Make random marks with their finger and some tools.
- Begin to use anticlockwise movement and retrace vertical lines.
- Begin to form recognizable letters.

Look, listen and note
How do they:
- make different marks?
- form recognizable letters or words?

Houses and homes

This chapter delights and intrigues us with imaginative play themed around traditional stories, hilarious nonsense rhymes, putting teddies to bed, guessing games and creating our own mysterious fantastical story about what lurks in the attic. We tune in our listening skills with crazy noisy fun in the kitchen and making a delicious sounds pie. We even explore animal homes and habitats with the delightful poem, 'Who am I?'

Chapter contents

Role-play area ideas

These role-play areas will provide a fun and meaningful learning context for all learners:

- bedroom
- kitchen
- house
- bathroom
- *Goldilocks and the Three Bears*
- *Three little pigs.*

Songs and rhymes

These song suggestions can be adapted by adding relevant places and children's names to add interest and relevance to the children:

- 'Polly put the kettle on'
- 'This is the house that Jack built'
- 'There was an old woman who lived in a shoe'
- 'I'm a little tea pot'.

Hands-on learning

Create an understanding of different homes by building outdoor dens, junk homes and incorporating different home role-play areas such as a caravan or hotel. Visit different houses in the local community such as bungalows or flats.

Parents as partners home activities

Recognize differences in what families define as a house or what they may call home. For example, travelling families may refer to their home as their ancestral origins. Some children may live in a flat, bungalow, cavaran or care home. Differences should be welcomed and embraced without pressuring children to discuss their home lives if they do not wish to.

Invite parents and carers to come and talk about how their homes and lives are different, and incorporate stories that recognize children's ethnical background in a positive light, for example discussing differences in houses and homes in other places in the world.

Encourage family members of children learning EAL to share their experiences of moving to a different home, learning a different language, making new friends and having new experiences.

Invite children to bring a bear from home when exploring the story *Goldilocks and the Three Bears*.

Links with the Early Learning Goals and EYFS

Personal, emotional and social development:

- Understand that people have different needs, views, cultures and beliefs that need to be treated with respect.
- Understand that they can expect others to treat their needs, views, cultures and beliefs with respect.

Knowledge and understanding of the world:

- Build and construct with a wide range of objects, selecting appropriate resources and adapting their work where necessary.
- Select the tools and techniques they need to shape, assemble and join materials they are using.
- Observe, find out about and identify features in the place they live and the natural world.
- Find out about their environment, and talk about those features they like and dislike.

Physical development:

- Handle tools, objects, construction and malleable materials safely and with increasing control.

Creative development:

- Express and communicate their ideas, thoughts and feelings by using a widening range of materials, suitable tools, imaginative role play, movement, designing and making and a variety of songs and musical instruments.
- Explore colour, texture, shape, form and space in two or three dimensions.
- Use their imagination in art and design, music, dance, role play and stories.

ACTIVITY 49
Crazy kitchen sounds

Vocabulary
shake, rattle, bang, crash, whizz, pop, ping

You will need
A collection of noise makers from the kitchen such as keys, clock, cutlery and utensils, baking trays, pots, pans and fizzy pop bottles.

You will also need
A home role-play area and role-play electrical appliances such as a microwave that pings or a toaster that pops and a screen (this could be created using a clothes horse and a large piece of fabric).

Online resources available

Introduce the session using the role-play kitchen area. Build anticipation and excitement by finding items from the kitchen and model how each item might be 'played'. Encourage the children to describe the contrasting sounds and explore the different objects.

Explain that you are going to make some kitchen sounds behind a screen for them to guess what they are. Make different sounds for the children to listen to, describe and name, for example unscrewing a pop bottle or rattling a bunch of keys. Let some of the children have a turn at making the sounds. Can they think of other sounds that they hear in the kitchen?

Meeting different learners' needs

Support some children to explore the different objects to create various sounds. Use picture cues such as photographs or symbols (see the 'Supporting children' section on pages 142–7) of the items used in the activity to provide them with a visual prompt to support their understanding and help them answer questions. Remove the screen for children with a hearing impairment.

Provide children learning EAL with time to observe the game before asking them to take their turn. Use simple language and visual cues to support their understanding as well as welcoming any verbal contributions to describe the sound. For example, their imitation of the sound of a microwave might be different from the sound made by others.

Challenge some children to use their phonic knowledge to link sounds to letters such as 'The spoon hits the pan and goes t, t, t'.

Learning steps
- Distinguish one sound from another.
- Show interest in play with sounds, songs and rhymes.
- Link sounds to letters, naming and sounding the letters of the alphabet.

Look, listen and note
How do they:
- communicate in different ways?
- describe and distinguish different sounds?
- use their phonic knowledge during the activity?

ACTIVITY 50
Sounds pie

Vocabulary
rhyme, sound, pie, stir, word, bowl, spoon

You will need
A large bowl, wooden spoon, large tin/pie dish.

You will also need
A collection of rhyming household objects or objects beginning with the same sound.

Online resources available

Display the objects on the floor in the centre of a circle of children. Invite each child to select an item, name it and add it to the bowl. Ask the children to listen for the common sound, either the initial letter sound for example 'p' for pen, pot, pan and so on (easier); or the rhyming final sound such as hat, cat, mat, bat (harder). After each turn, stir the contents and sing the following song:

(Sung to the tune of 'Row, row, row your boat')
Stir, stir, stir the pie,
Stir it round and round.
Add a ... bat ... a cat ... a hat ...
And stir it round and round.

Once each child has added an item to the pie transfer the contents into a pie dish. Pretend to bake it in the oven before sharing it out among the children.

Meeting different learners' needs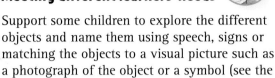

Support some children to explore the different objects and name them using speech, signs or matching the objects to a visual picture such as a photograph of the object or a symbol (see the 'Supporting children' section on pages 142–7).

Provide children learning EAL with time to observe the game before asking them to take their turn. Use simple language and visual cues to support their understanding while encouraging them to model simple language and echo the names of different objects.

Challenge some children to generate rhyming strings and sing the song using other rhyming household objects such as tap, cap, map and so on.

Learning steps
- Distinguish one sound from another.
- Enjoy rhyming and rhythmic activities.
- Show an awareness of rhyme and alliteration.
- Continue a rhyming string.
- Hear and say sounds in words in the order in which they occur.

Look, listen and note
How do they:
- communicate in different ways?
- recognize and identify the sound at the beginning and end of words?

ACTIVITY 51

Who am I?

Vocabulary
poem, home, verse, pattern, creature, animal

You will need

An enlarged copy of the poem in this activity, a large piece of blue material, strips of green tissue paper, twigs, leaves, branches, home role-play area, objects from the shed, old junk material and fabric for the children to create animal 'dens', and photographs of a bird, fish, spider and a person.

Online resources available

Ask the children to think about different creatures and where they live. Encourage them to think about their habitats such as a pond, tree, shed and so on. Read aloud the poem, 'Who am I?' Invite the children to join in with the repeated lines used in the poem and predict which creature each verse is about.

Ask the children to make different habitats from the poem using the props provided. For example, use a large blue piece of material and strips of green tissue paper to create the sea. Ask the children to take on the role of different creatures and move to where they would live. Ask the question, 'Who lives up on the branch? 'The child perched on the twigs stands up and says, 'I do, this is my home.' Ensure that each child has a turn.

Who am I?

Who am I?
Hiding in the garden shed,
Can you see my little web?
I am a spider,
This is my home.

Who am I?
My nest is high up in the tree,
Singing is the life for me,
I am a bird,
This is my home.

Who am I?
Swimming in the deep blue sea,
Blowing bubbles one, two, three,
I am a fish,
This is my home.

Who am I?
Where I eat, and play and rest,
My home's the one I love the best,
I am me,
This is my home.

Meeting different learners' needs

Use toy animals, photographs of different animal homes and objects linked to each habitat to support children's understanding. For example, explore a picture of a pond, a toy fish and shallow tray of water for the verse about living in the sea. This multi-sensory activity will make the session more meaningful and will add interest for some children.

Provide children learning EAL with time to listen to the poem several times. The repeated structure of the poem is an effective way of helping them to remember whole sentences by tuning into the rhythm that accompanies them.

Challenge some children to make up some new verses to the poem using the same structure and rhythm of the poem.

Learning steps
- Show an interest in stories, songs and rhymes.
- Listen and join in with stories and poems, one to one and also in small groups.
- Suggest how a verse in a poem might end.
- Explore and experiment with sounds, words and texts.

Look, listen and note
How do they:
- respond to the poem you read with them?
- recognize and talk about the structure of the poem?

ACTIVITY 52
What's in the attic?

Vocabulary
treasure chest, lock, attic, upstairs

You will need

A trunk or an old box, persona dolls, dressing-up clothes, examples of different illustrations or characters, talcum powder, interesting objects placed inside the box such as a letter, map, costume jewellery, key, wand and so on.

Introduce the chest to the group and talk about what it is. Explain that you found it hidden in the attic and it must have been there for a very long time as it is covered in dust. Tap the lid to send talc up into the air.

Brainstorm ideas about who it might belong to, what might be inside the chest and how it came to be in the attic. Use the ideas to form the beginning of a story by scribing simple sentences and keywords on a white board.

Invite the children to open the box and discover what is inside. Continue to develop the story using the children's imaginative ideas. Ask them to illustrate the story by drawing the character they believe the chest belongs to. This could be an imaginary character or someone they know. Support the children to add a short caption or label to their picture. Retell the story generated from the children's ideas using their illustrations and shared writing.

Meeting different learners' needs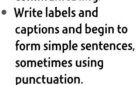

Support some children by providing visual cues and acting out different children's ideas using gestures and objects from the chest as props. For children who are not able to produce a drawing, support them to choose from a selection of pre-cut characters from magazines and photocopied book illustrations to create their character.

For children learning EAL use persona dolls and props to support their understanding of different characters.

Challenge some children to write simple sentences about their character.

Learning steps
- Sometimes give meaning to the marks they make.
- Use writing as a means of recording and communicating.
- Write labels and captions and begin to form simple sentences, sometimes using punctuation.

Look, listen and note
How do they:
- talk about the marks they make?
- make use of phonic knowledge as they attempt to write words and simple sentences?

ACTIVITY 53
Three little pigs

You will need
A copy of the story *The Three Little Pigs* along with the following props: a handful of straw, a brick, small sticks, three soft toy/model pigs and a wolf, an electric fan and a model house.
Online resources available

Vocabulary
house, straw, brick, wood, puffed, huffed, blew, pig, wolf

Share the story, *The Three Little Pigs*, using the props over several sessions with the children until they become familiar with the structure and language used in the book. Focus on creating an atmosphere using your voice, expressions and gestures. For example, pause, lower your tone and speak slowly to build anticipation while raising your voice and talking hurriedly to create a sense of urgency. Use different voices for the characters in the book such as, a deep gruff voice for the wolf and a squeaky frightened voice for the little pigs.

Talk about how the story makes the children feel. Are they excited, scared, nervous? Ask them how they feel about the characters. Encourage the children to express their feelings and ideas using their facial expressions, words and actions.

Ask the children to change the story by thinking of new modern characters. For example, the big bad wolf might be a giant green alien. Retell the story using the new characters inviting the children to join in.

Meeting different learners' needs

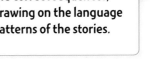

Use the sensory objects to bring the story to life and give added meaning for children who need greater support. Help children who find it difficult to talk about emotions by providing photographs/symbols (see the 'Supporting children' section on pages 142–7) of emotions for them model their expressions on.

Children learning EAL will benefit from the varying tone of your voice as well as the use of your expressions and gestures to accompany the story. Persona dolls or emotion puppets can be used to support the children when talking about how the characters feel.

Challenge some children to retell the story using their new characters, drawing on the language patterns and sequence of the original story.

Learning steps
- Show an interest in stories, songs and rhymes.
- Begin to be aware of the way stories are structured.
- Explore and experiment with sounds, words and texts.
- Retell narratives in the correct sequences, drawing on the language patterns of the stories.

Look, listen and note
How do they:
- respond to the story and express their ideas?
- use familiar story language to retell their story such as 'Once upon a time'?
- demonstrate an understanding of the elements of the story?

ACTIVITY 54
House mimes

Vocabulary
pretend, copy, act, house, actions

You will need
Home role-play area and a range of role-play props such as an ironing board, an iron, a pile of clothes, a tea set and so on, A5 pieces of card each displaying a different action picture/word linked with the home. For example, dusting, washing, ironing, vacuuming and so on.

Online resources available

Introduce the activity using the home role-play area. Explain to the children that they are going to play a pretending game. Explore different objects from the role-play area and invite the children to suggest what each item might be used for.

Show the children the action cards and read out a few examples. Demonstrate to the children how to act out the action through mime (without speech) both with props (easier) and without (harder). Ask each child to select a card and help them to read the words on it. The child must then act out the actions while the others guess what it says.

Meeting different learners' needs

Support children in this activity by providing them with props to help them when acting out their action card. Also use picture cues such as photographs relating to the activities to provide them with ideas when guessing what the other children are doing.

For children learning EAL, recognize non-verbal communication, praise it and respond to it positively. Using the home role-play area will provide a meaningful context to support the children's understanding of the activity.

Challenge some children to mime different actions linked to the home without using an action card for ideas and without using props.

Learning steps
- Use actions, sometimes with limited talk, that are largely connected with the 'here and now'.
- Use language as a powerful means of widening contacts, sharing feelings, experiences and thoughts.
- Use language to imagine and recreate roles and experiences.

Look, listen and note
How do they:
- use actions to support and think about what they are doing?
- use gesture and intonation to convey meaning?

ACTIVITY 55
Send a postcard

You will need

Examples of different postcards from various destinations, blank postcards, a selection of writing and colouring tools, stamps, a post box (this could be a painted shoe box with a rectangular hole cut into the lid).

Online resources available

> **Vocabulary**
> write, postcard, send, receive, stamp, address, message

Introduce this activity by asking a colleague to deliver a post bag filled with different examples of old postcards brought in by the children. Read the different postcards looking at the pictures and drawing their attention to the common features of a postcard such as a stamp, address, picture and message.

Invite the children to talk about their experiences of holidays and travel. Encourage them to think about different reasons for travelling away from home, such as to celebrate a religious festival, to visit family living in a different country or to go on holiday. Ask them to create a postcard to send home encouraging them to add a picture and 'writing'. Also encourage them to add a stamp, write the address and send their postcard by posting it into the letter box. Support the children to form letters correctly using a pencil.

Meeting different learners' needs

Support the children by praising their attempts at 'writing', which may be random mark making, and encourage them to develop fine manipulation skills when adding a stamp and posting their postcard.

This activity provides a great opportunity to invite the parents and carers of children learning EAL to send in postcards from home displaying print in different languages and from places significant to the child.

Challenge some children to write words or a simple message on their postcard, taking care to form letters correctly.

Learning steps
- Use one-handed tools and equipment.
- Manipulate objects with increasing control.
- Begin to form recognizable letters.
- Use a pencil and hold it effectively to form recognizable letters, most of which are correctly formed.

Look, listen and note
How do they:
- control equipment and writing tools?
- make marks and talk about their writing?
- form recognizable letters independently?

ACTIVITY 56
Time for bed

Vocabulary
teddy, bed, night, sleep, pyjamas

You will need
A selection of teddies of varying sizes, a small, medium and large bed (these can be made using boxes and pieces of material), pyjamas for the teddies to wear (old baby clothes work well), the book *Goldilocks and the Three Bears*, relaxing music, a bed-time story book.

Read the story, *Goldilocks and the Three Bears*, with the children. Explain that they are going to get the teddies ready for bed and settle them down to sleep. Ask them to work together to decide what they must do to get the teddies ready for bed.

Encourage the children to share their personal experiences of going to bed, for example do they enjoy a story before they go to bed? Also support the children to negotiate and solve problems using communication such as, 'Oh dear, Daddy Bear doesn't fit in the little bed, who could sleep in the little bed?' Ensure that the children have plenty of opportunities to engage in communication without adult support.

Meeting different learners' needs

Support some children to interact with others using gestures, facial expressions and actions. Encourage the children to listen to each other as well as an adult leader and to follow simple instructions during play.

It may take time for children learning EAL to understand and recognize representational play. Provide them with the opportunity to play and explore the objects and props, encouraging them to 'talk' about what the objects are and could be used for.

Challenge some children to make up their own story using the characters from the story *Goldilocks and the Three Bears*.

Learning steps
- Listen to others in one-to-one or small groups when conversation interests them.
- Initiate conversation, attend to and take account of what others say.
- Interact with others, negotiating plans and activities and taking turns in conversation.
- Listen with enjoyment and respond to stories, songs and other music, rhymes and poems, and make up their own stories, songs, rhymes and poems.

Look, listen and note
How do they:
- use their preferred language and how has this developed?
- engage and take turns in conversation?
- concentrate on what others have said and respond appropriately?
- speak clearly and confidently and show an awareness of the listener?

ACTIVITY 57
Hey diddle fiddle

Vocabulary
poem, nonsense, funny, rhyme

You will need
The copy of the poem 'Hey diddle diddle' written onto a wipe board, wipeboard pens, a toy cat, cow and dog, a photograph of or toy fiddle, dish and spoon, a picture of the moon, pairs of rhyming household objects such as a tin and pin, a tap and cap and so on, a selection of other toy animals, for example mouse, hamster and horse.
Online resources available

Read the poem with the children and explore the related objects. Create humour and laughter by talking about each verse, asking the children questions and discussing how it does not make sense. For example, 'Would a cow be able to jump over the moon?'

Use the wipe board and pens to demonstrate how to change some nouns to create a new nonsense rhyme. Invite the children to suggest different animals or objects using props or their imagination. For example:

Hey diddle diddle, the hamster and the fiddle,
The horse jumped over the pin.
The little mouse laughed to see such fun
And the dish ran away with the tin!

Meeting different learners' needs

Support children in this activity by inviting them to explore and name a selection of household objects before acting out parts of the rhyme, for example jumping a toy cow over a moon.

Children with autism or those learning EAL may find this activity quite abstract and difficult to grasp. Provide them with time to observe and avoid asking them to take their turn first.

Challenge some children to suggest pairs of rhyming household objects, either using the objects or from their own ideas.

Learning steps

- Begin to experiment with words and sounds.
- Use language for an increasing range of purposes.
- Listen with enjoyment, and respond to stories, songs and other music, rhymes and poems, and make up their own stories, songs, rhymes and poems.

Look, listen and note

How do they:

- use gestures and body language to communicate?
- act out rhymes and stories?
- make up their own nonsense rhyme?

ACTIVITY 58
Let's play Goldilocks!

You will need
A copy of the story
*Goldilocks and the Three
Bears* and related objects including
a doll (Goldilocks), three bears
of various sizes, three bowls and
spoons, three different sized chairs,
three boxes and blankets to be used
as beds, home role-play area.

Vocabulary
feelings, emotions, happy, sad, angry, worried

Read the story *Goldilocks and the Three Bears*
with the children until they are familiar with the
sequence of events and characters. Talk together
about the story and encourage the children to identify with how the different
bears might have felt. For example, Mummy Bear might have been angry while
Baby Bear may have felt sad. Ask the children to reflect on their own experiences.
Have they ever felt angry or sad?

Encourage the children to use the props and home role-play area to re-enact
the story for themselves. Encourage them to express different emotions through
gestures, body language, speech and facial expressions.

Meetings different learners' needs

Support the children in this activity by inviting them to take on the role of Goldilocks and to talk about what they are doing and what is happening to them. Use props, gestures and actions to support their communication and focus on language concerned with the 'here and now'. For example, 'I'm eating the porridge'.

Value non-verbal communications from children learning EAL and sensitively demonstrate pronunciation and ordering of words to children rather than correcting them.

Challenge some children to talk through their actions explaining what they are doing as they act out their stories. Encourage them to develop a storyline with their own ideas.

Learning steps
- Use actions, sometimes with limited talk, that are largely connected with the 'here and now'.
- Begin to use talk instead of action to rehearse, reorder and reflect on past experience, linking significant events from their own experience and from stories, paying attention to how events lead into one another.
- Use language to imagine and recreate roles and experiences.
- Use talk to organize, sequence and clarify thinking, ideas, feelings and events.

Look, listen and note
How do they:

- use gesture, actions and some talk to support what they are doing?
- use talk to reflect upon, clarify, sequence and think about present and past experiences, ideas and feelings?
- use their dominant language in play?

ACTIVITY 59
Bedroom name plaques

Vocabulary
name, write, letter, copy

You will need

Tough thick card cut into rectangular plaques, examples of name plaques, texture/foam letters (upper and lower case), PVA glue, glue spreaders, pencils, thick marker pens, shallow flat trays, various textured creative materials such as glitter, sand, small beads, sequins, pencil shavings, small buttons, rice and so on.

Explain that the children will be making a name plaque for their bedroom door and show some examples. Invite the children to practise mark-making in trays filled with various materials using their finger. Encourage some children to write letters in the trays by copying or drawing around letter outlines, for example writing an 's' in a tray filled with glitter.

Ask the children to write their name onto a blank plaque. Demonstrate how to trace over their writing using a glue stick spreader adding different textured materials to the glue to create a touch-and-feel name plaque. Once the plaques are dry ask the children to close their eyes and help them to trace their finger around different letters, encouraging them to identify letters and sounds.

Meeting different learners' needs

Some children may find it difficult to write letters independently or to identify the letters in their name. Encourage these children to explore the resources using their hands and fingers to make random marks in the materials. Help them to trace over texture letters and your writing.

Visual support is vital for children learning EAL as well as writing their name correctly.

Challenge some children to write signs for other rooms in the house.

Learning steps
- Make random marks with their fingers and some tools.
- Begin to form recognizable letters.
- Use a pencil and hold it effectively to form recognizable letters, most of which are correctly formed.

Look, listen and note
How do they:
- make different marks when writing?
- control equipment and materials?
- attempt to write their name?

ACTIVITY 60
My home

Vocabulary
label, write, house, model

Explain that the children are going to be making
and labelling a model of their house or the place that they live. Explore examples of labels such as named work trays, labelled equipment and labels and signs in their environment. Once the children are familiar with the concept of a label give each child a shoe box and explain that this will be their house or place where they live.

Support the children to construct a house using various resources. Encourage them to talk about the people who live in their house, welcoming differences and similarities among children. Help them to create labels for the different features of their house or place where they live such as the roof and garden as well as labelling model people and animals for their family members and pets.

Meeting different learners' needs

Some children may find it difficult to write labels independently. Encourage these children to ascribe meaning to the marks that they add to their model, for example by colouring in the garden or talking about what they have drawn. Support them to write labels or use symbols as labels (see the 'Supporting children' section on pages 142–7).

For children learning EAL, use a picture of their own home or place that they live to develop their understanding of the activity. Welcome contributions that show diversity in children's experiences of who lives at home.

Challenge some children to write phonetically plausible attempts at short captions about their home such as 'My bedrum is pinc'.

Learning steps
- Distinguish between the marks they make.
- Sometimes give meaning to marks as they draw and paint.
- Ascribe meaning to marks that they see in different places.
- Write labels and captions.

Look, listen and note
How do they:
- talk about the marks they have made?
- give meaning to the marks they have made?
- attempt to write labels using their 'writing'?
- use phonic knowledge to write simple words or short sentences?

Supporting children – additional information

This section aims to provide further information for supporting some children in your class. It is important to recognize that it is hard to generalize the needs of children with specific learning requirements and that no two children are the same. It is advisable to use this book in conjunction with specialist advice and provision. Links to organizations, resources and specialists are provided in the 'Further reading and information' section of this book on pages 148–9.

For children who are learning English as an additional language (EAL):

- Visual support is vital for EAL children such as visual words, text and labels.
- Use books, posters and role-play items that display a variety of scripts to support language awareness.
- Use picture communication symbols and boards to provide children with visual pictures to support text to help children's understanding. These can be created using software such as Boardmaker or Communicate in Print (see the 'Further reading and information' section to find information about these Widgit products as well as links to other products for symbol communication and literacy support).
- Use songs and stories recorded in home language and placed in a rest area for children to have time out. It can be very tiring to listen for long periods to a language you do not understand.
- Recognize non-verbal communication, praise it and respond to it positively.
- Provide first-hand experiences.
- Dual-text stories can be a good resource where home languages have a written text and parents and carers are literate in that language.
- Choose stories with a clear story line, written or told in simple direct language.
- Learn a few keywords in a child's home language such as, 'look' and 'listen' and use when appropriate.
- Songs and rhymes are a good way of helping children to remember whole sentences/phrases by tuning into the rhythm that accompanies them.
- Children sharing the same first language should not be discouraged from sharing that language together in play. Instead this should be facilitated where possible, for example with the support and help of the parents and carers.

For children with dyslexia:

- Use clear and simple sentences and instructions as they may have difficulties processing language.
- Use visual cards and objects during activities to support their short-term memory.
- Use objects and prompt cards to support children with sequencing activities.
- Provide children with time to think about their answers as they find it difficult to produce mental or written answers quickly.
- Use a multi-sensory approach with plenty of opportunity for repetition and consolidation when learning letters and sounds as they may find this difficult to grasp.
- Children may find it difficult to visualize and grasp rhyming words and patterns, so use word cards or a wipe board to visually compare words.
- Bear in mind that dyslexic children find it difficult to learn things 'by heart'.
- Provide support when reading unusual words.

For children with speech and language difficulties:

- Where appropriate use individual symbols and symbol boards to provide children with pictures to accompany text to support their understanding and communication. Symbols are different from pictures as each symbol focuses on a single concept. Symbols can be put together to give more precise information. This is unlike a picture, such as an illustration in a book, which can be interpreted in different ways and contains a combination of information. Symbols can be created using software such as Boardmaker or Communicate in Print (see the 'Further reading and information' section to find information about these Widgit products as well as links to other products for symbol communication and literacy support).

- Use recording devices such as a *Big Mac* switch or a *Step-by-Step* (see the 'Further reading and information' section on pages 148–9 for manufacturers). These devices enable adults to record simple messages or responses for children with speech and language difficulties to use to support their contribution in group sessions. They are designed to be easily accessible for a range of children and give an easily re-recordable voice output. They can be used in a number of ways, such as to contribute in discussions, share news in circle time, control a simple game, give an instruction to other children or participate in story telling. For example, during the story *The Gingerbread Man*, a child could take on the role of the main character and join in with story telling by pressing a switch with the pre-recorded message, 'Run, run as fast as you can, you can't catch me I'm the Gingerbread Man', repeated throughout the story.
- Recognize and reward children for using a range of communication strategies such as gestures, actions, signing and eye-contact.
- Use clear and simple sentences and instructions, without speaking overly fast or slow but speaking as you usually would.
- Children may have some difficulty using language in context, for example problems with listening, turn-taking and sharing conversations. Support and teach them and their peers to use communication other than speech to communicate, such as gestures, actions and signing. Opportunities for interaction and turn-taking should be provided.
- Encourage all the children to engage in miming activities to develop their awareness and understanding of communicating in ways other than speech alone.
- Where appropriate, use sign language such as British Sign Language or Makaton to support children's understanding. Link with parents, carers or specialists to provide signing classes for all the children to support both adults and children when communicating with others with speech and language difficulties.

For children with gross motor difficulties:

- Provide children with time to organize their movements and support them to carry out actions from their own intentions rather than doing things for them.
- It may be difficult for children to participate in some activities such as putting up their hand, accessing the role-play area or joining in with actions songs and

rhymes. Find other ways that children with gross motor difficulties can join in with everyone else, for example nodding their head instead of raising their hand. Adapt the role-play area by considering how it can be made accessible by everyone including those in wheelchairs.

- Ensure the children are in a good seating position to ensure optimal access and independence opportunities.
- Some children may have specialist equipment such as standing frames and supported chairs. Ensure that this does not segregate them from the other children by providing opportunities for children to play on a similar level to promote interaction with others.
- Plan how children will access an activity before setting it up, for example if they are unable to access water-play in a standing position, invite a small group of children to play with a smaller water tray at a table or on their wheelchair tray.
- Switch accessible toys and resources are available which can be used in games and activities by all learners but also provide children with access difficulties with an activity in which they can be more independent (see the 'Further reading and information' section on pages 148–9 for links to suppliers).

For children with fine motor difficulties:

- Use pencil grips, sticky-tac or Dycem matting (a rubber sheet placed on a table/work surface) to help to keep paper, cards, books and objects from slipping around on the table.
- Try to reduce the amount of written recording that children have to do as this can be very time-consuming and frustrating. Find alternative ways of recording such as using symbols such as Bliss TEACCH, Writing with Symbols, Mayor Johnson or Braille. Other examples include: video recording, photographs, scribing their dictation to a helper, specialist ICT such as accessible keyboards, and software which uses symbols such as Clicker and Close-Pro (see the 'Further reading and information' section on pages 148–9).
- Provide the children with sufficient time and opportunity to produce written work, welcoming and rewarding any mark-making they produce.
- Support the children to explore objects if they find it difficult to do so for themselves.
- Use objects, writing tools and equipment that are easier to pick up and hold onto, such as thick pens and crayons.
- Some children may find it difficult to execute movements that involve crossing the mid-line of their bodies so bear this in mind when you ask them to engage in an activity.
- Switch accessible toys and resources are available which can be used in games and activities by all learners but also provide children with access difficulties with an activity in which they can be more independent (see the 'Further reading and information' section on pages 148–9 for links to suppliers).

For children who are visually impaired (this may include children with partial sight loss to children who are blind):

- Use images that display clear non-busy images and text. For example, enlarge pages from textbooks and use bold print.
- Provide children with their own set of objects as it may take them longer to explore.
- Give time for processing information and completion of a task.
- Ensure text and pictures have a good visual contrast such as black on yellow or white paper. Some children may have a preferred contrast.
- Sometimes illustrations may need extra definition by using a thicker outline.
- Black print on white paper can create a glare effect, but by using good positioning which avoids lighting problems, photocopying onto pastel A4 paper or by laminating with a matt overlay this glare is reduced.
- Using the access options on the computer, increase the size and definition of icons for word processing.
- All auditory experiences should be accompanied by concrete first-hand experiences such as exploring props which accompany a story while reading a book.
- Use bigger, bolder, brighter and wider character spacing of words as well as using spaces between lines for reading.
- Use all the main senses (smell, taste, visual, tactile and kinesthetic) where possible.
- Children may find it difficult to use a range of communication strategies in play, especially role play, such as reading other facial expressions and body language. Support play by talking through what is happening and encouraging others to vary their speaking style during role play to convey further meaning.

For children with hearing impairments (this may include children with partial or temporary hearing loss due to glue or swimmer's ear or children who are deaf):

- Ensure that children are directly facing you (and a signer if they have one).
- Use visual cues such as signing, gestures, photographs and pictures as well as using kinesthetic learning resources.
- Where appropriate, link with parents and carers or specialists to provide signing classes for all the children to support both adults and children when communicating with others with hearing difficulties.
- Where appropriate, use individual symbols and symbol boards to provide children with pictures to accompany text to support their understanding and communication. Symbols are different from pictures as each symbol focuses on a single concept. Symbols can be put together to give more precise information. This is unlike a picture, such as an illustration in a book, which can be interpreted in different ways and contains a combination of information. Symbols can be created using software such as Board maker or Writing with Symbol (see the 'Further reading and information' section on pages 148–9 for links to websites and suppliers).

- Provide time to process instructions and questions.
- Demonstrate techniques and ensure that children can see each other.
- Children may rely on signing systems to support understanding of written and spoken/signed words.
- Visual colour coding and organization may be used to support their understanding of spelling and building sentences.
- Establish and maintain eye contact and vary your voice, facial expressions and gestures to engage the learner.
- Do not shout as this can distort the lips; speak at a normal speed and volume.
- Keep background noise to a minimum.
- When talking in a group encourage the speaker to raise his or her hand to make conversations easier to follow.
- Use simple games to develop conversation skills such as turn-taking and incorporate simple signs (colour dominos, picture lotto or snap).
- Encourage all the children to use various facial expressions and use role play to support the understanding of children with hearing communication difficulties.

For children with autism (this may include children with varied ability ranging from completely non-verbal to children with Asperger's syndrome who often have a very high IQ):

- Some children may find social interaction, shared learning and play difficult, and will require an adult or peers to model appropriate behaviours and language.
- Support and encourage social interactions with other peers during play.
- Some children may find it difficult to attribute thoughts, beliefs and actions to others during role play and discussion. This will need to be modelled and explained to them.
- Some children may find group work difficult and should be able to be on the periphery of the group, joining in as their confidence develops.
- Children may appear confident with an area of learning in one context but find it difficult to generalize their ideas. Situations must be provided for concepts to be taught together through cross-curricular learning.
- Children may find using picture cues difficult as they are unable to see the connection between the illustration and what it is supposed to represent. Use precise language when discussing pictures and use photographs as well as real objects to support their understanding.
- Some children with autism prefer quiet activities rather than bouncy hectic ones. If the activity is lively, create a quiet area where an autistic child can work with just a few children in a calmer, low-arousal environment.

Further reading and information

www.1voice.info – A network and support for children and families using communication aids

www.ace-centre.org.uk – ACE Centre (supporting individuals with speech and language difficulties)

www.afasic.org.uk – An organisation to help children and young people with speech and language impairments and their families

www.arcos.org.uk – ARCOS is a national charity that works with children and adults who have communication and eating (swallowing) difficulties, their families, carers and others involved

www.autism.org.uk – The National Autistic Society

www.nas.org.uk – The National Autistic Society

www.bagbooks.org – multi-sensory stories sacks

www.batod.org.uk – The British Association of Teachers of the Deaf (BATOD)

www.bdadyslexia.org.uk – British Dyslexia Association

www.btbetterworld.com – A programme concerned with the development of core communication skills for all children. This site contains some excellent resources to develop inclusive communication development such as 'The Cookbook'

www.calibre.org.uk – Calibre story tape lending library

www.clearvisionproject.org – Clearvision is a UK postal lending library of mainstream children's books with added Braille

www.communicationmatters.org.uk – Communication Matters is a UK national charitable organisation of members concerned with the augmentative and alternative communication (AAC) needs of people with complex communication needs

www.cricksoft.com – Crick Software (specialist software and resources to support children with SEN)

www.dyslexiaaction.org.uk – Dyslexia Action

www.ican.org.uk – I CAN (national educational charity for children with speech and language difficulties)

www.inclusion.ngfl.gov.uk – National Grid for Learning (NGFL) (the SEN Inclusion website on the National Grid for Learning provides an interactive online catalogue of teaching materials and sources of information for mainstream teachers who have children with special educational needs in their class. This site is also highly motivational and full of fun teaching material for all learners)

www.inclusive.co.uk – Inclusive Technology (SEN software, switches and computer access devices, communication aids and assistive technology for children with physical disabilities, sensory impairment or learning difficulties)

www.languageforlearning.co.uk – Language for Learning is all about working together to support children with language and communication difficulties in mainstream classrooms and early years' settings

www.mayer-johnson.com – Mayer-Johnson (information and resources on symbol communication and literacy support. Symbols are suitable for aiding a range of learners including children with memory difficulties, dyslexia, dyspraxia, hearing difficulties and autistic spectrum disorder. Symbols can also be used to support children learning English as an additional language and young children who are not yet reading)

www.nagcbritain.org.uk – National Association for Gifted and Talented Children

www.nbcs.org.uk – National Blind Children's Society

www.ndcs.org.uk – National Deaf Children's Society

www.pri-liberator.com – Software, switches and computer access devices, communication aids and assistive technology for children with physical disabilities, sensory impairment or learning difficulties

www.rnib.org.uk – Royal National Institute of Blind People

www.rnib.org.uk/library – Royal National Institute of Blind People (lending library)

www.rnid.org.uk –Royal National Institute for Deaf People (RNID)

www.signalong.org.uk – An example of a sign-supporting system based on British Sign Language, designed to help children and adults with communication difficulties, mostly associated with learning disabilities that is user-friendly for easy access

www.sparklebox.co.uk – Early Years and KS1 free resources

www.stammering.org – Information and support on stammering, also known as stuttering

www.standards.dfes.gov.uk – The Standards Website (provides links to The Early Years Foundation Stage curriculum, information on developing teaching and learning in the early years, supporting children learning EAL, SEN and gifted and talented children)

www.teachernet.gov.uk/teachingandlearning/EYFS – (teaching support and information in the early years foundation stage)

www.treehouse.org.uk – The TreeHouse Trust supports families and practitioners working with children with Autism

www.vistablind.org.uk – VISTA (visual impairment and special needs advice)

www.widgit.com – WIDGIT (information and resources on symbol communication and literacy support. Symbols are suitable for aiding a range of learners including children with memory difficulties, dyslexia, dyspraxia, hearing difficulties and autistic spectrum disorder. Symbols can also be used to support children learning English as an additional language and young children who are not yet reading)